The
Magick
of
Birthdays

The
Magick
of
Birthdays

Rituals, Spells, and Recipes
for Honoring Your Solar Return

＊

Hannah Hawthorn

A TarcherPerigee Book

tarcherperigee

an imprint of Penguin Random House LLC
penguinrandomhouse.com

Most TarcherPerigee books are available at special quantity discounts for bulk
purchase for sales promotions, premiums, fund-raising, and educational needs.
Special books or book excerpts also can be created to fit specific needs.
For details, write: SpecialMarkets@penguinrandomhouse.com.

Library of Congress Cataloging-in-Publication Data

Names: Hawthorn, Hannah, author.
Title: The magick of birthdays: rituals, spells, and recipes for
honoring your solar return / Hannah Hawthorn.
Description: New York: TarcherPerigee, Penguin Random House LLC, 2022. |
Includes bibliographical references.
Identifiers: LCCN 2022003580 (print) | LCCN 2022003581 (ebook) |
ISBN 9780593538531 (trade paperback) | ISBN 9780593538548 (epub)
Subjects: LCSH: Birthdays—Miscellanea. | Astrology. | Incantations. | Charms. | Magic.
Classification: LCC BF1729.B45 H39 2022 (print) | LCC BF1729.B45 (ebook) |
DDC 133.5/4042—dc23/eng/20220215
LC record available at https://lccn.loc.gov/2022003580
LC ebook record available at https://lccn.loc.gov/2022003581

Printed in the United States of America
1st Printing

Interior art courtesy of Shutterstock.com and Clipart.com
Book design by Laura K. Corless

This book is dedicated to divinity,
however we may see or call it.

CONTENTS

Part I
Astrological Magic

Part II
Candle Magic

Part III
The Witch's Birthday Party

Bewitched

If I think back far enough, I can remember my fifth birthday. I was sitting on an oversized wooden chair in my grandparents' dining room, my legs far too short to touch the floor. On the table in front of me was a cake topped with five small lit candles. My eyes were entranced with their flames, watching as the wax rolled down onto the frosting. Cheerfully surrounding me, my family was singing along to the tune of "Happy Birthday." As the song came to a close, they encouraged me to blow out the candles and make a wish. Being in kindergarten at the time, I'm positive I said something along the lines of "Art supplies!" or "New shoes!" I don't quite remember if these came to fruition, but I do remember that moment felt magical . . . and it was. Unbeknownst to me, I had just cast my first spell.

I would remain a stranger to witchcraft and ritual for many years after this experience. Like most of you reading, I'm sure, these were tales of fantasy and words reserved for the fiction found in the pages of Harry Potter. However, in the time between then and now, I have experienced many enchanting moments that led me to become the witch I am today. It would probably surprise you really, the number of things that are inadvertently "witchy." Collecting pennies and clovers for luck. Wishing on dandelions, eyelashes, and shooting stars. Not opening umbrellas inside, walking under ladders, or splitting the pole. Breaking wishbones and kissing under the mistletoe. Much like we wish on birthday candles, these events go unnoticed, but there were many times in my "Muggle" life that I experienced real magic.* This is because magic is constantly surrounding every one of us, weaved into the seemingly mundane aspects of our everyday life. Becoming aware of these things and seeking them out on purpose is what makes us witches.

When I discovered that wishing on birthday candles was spellwork, it lit a fire under me and changed my life trajectory completely. I thought to myself, *If this one small action is magic, what else is the universe hiding?* This sent me on a lifelong path of discovering everything I could about living a more magical life, which ultimately brought me here and is the reason this book came to be in your possession. My journey into witchcraft has felt a lot like falling down a rabbit hole. You start searching for answers about something as simple as birthday candles, and where you end up is entirely different. You could say that it was birthdays that truly bewitched me with their wonderfully enchanting yet confusing rituals. We give gifts, sing songs, spank each other, and light cakes on fire. Have you ever considered how truly peculiar they are? (If you're not from a place where birthday spankings exist, you are probably very confused

---

*As it appears in the title of the book, "magick" is spelled with a *k*. Within the occult community, this extra letter is used to differentiate between fantasy (magic) and real witchcraft (magick). However, going forward I will be dropping the *k*, as it feels redundant to repeat throughout the book when the title has already established the context we will be working in.

at this moment, but just consider yourself lucky.) These strange modern-day traditions didn't come to exist by accident. They are the result of thousands of years of accumulated magic.

This book may be called *The Magick of Birthdays*, but you will find far more than that here. This is a practical guide to become your own holiday and harness your personal power. Although you only have one birthday, in these pages, you will find the tools to work with that energy all year long and add an entirely new dimension to your practice. The information in this book is written from an astrological and magical perspective. We will unravel how birthdays came to be and use that as a foundation to celebrate in a way that is meaningful to us today. We will take those birthday candles and perform powerful candle magic. You will learn the basics of traditional astrology and how to read your natal chart as a tool for guidance. You'll learn planetary timing so you can live your life in sync with the celestial bodies. You'll utilize your solar return and work with the Sun and solar deities. You'll find spells and rituals, correspondence lists, and even magical birthday cake recipes.

This book was written for all experience levels and all types of magical practices. No prior knowledge is needed for you to understand anything we'll cover. I wrote this book for anyone with a birthday. The concepts are intended to be presented so both the beginner and experienced practitioner will see them in a new light. Take this information and integrate it into your practice in the

Birthdays are a powerful tool.

way that feels most natural to you. As witches, we often follow the earth's cycles and seasons, yet we ignore our own. Birthdays are a powerful tool, and I hope they create a space for you to pull and draw inspiration from. You can think of this book as a means to add depth to your craft or pioneer your magical journey. I don't intend for you to read this once and then set it on a shelf for eternity. This is a reference book to return to. Write in it. Dog-ear the pages. They are yours.

✴ DIVINELY CHOSEN BY THE COSMOS ✴

You're scrambling, hastily stuffing your belongings into your bag. You have to meet up with a friend soon, you're already running late, and it hits you. "Where are my keys?" You put down your things and begin turning your home inside out. All the couch cushions are on the floor, you've dumped out your bins, and now you're looking in the washing machine. Then your phone rings. It's presumably the person you're meeting asking where you are. You reach your hand into your bag to answer, and to your delighted dismay, you feel your keys. They were in your bag the entire time.

We've all been in this situation, when the thing you are looking for is right in front of you but you are looking everywhere else. Psychologists have been trying to understand this mental blind spot for decades. It's a metaphorical *scotoma*, defined as "a partial loss of vision or a blind spot in an otherwise normal field view." This unfortunate phenomenon spreads far and wide into all areas of life. In many ways, we are ignorant of all the glaringly obvious things staring back at us. Many of our greatest assets are right beside us, but we are too distracted to know they exist.

One of these forgotten familiar things is birthdays. We experience them every year, and everyone has one, so they aren't rare or sought after. You might not find too much importance in them. After all, they're just anniversaries of something you can't even remember. When you look at it that way, you won't pay them too much mind. They don't feel very meaningful. It's not your fault you feel that way. The world does a great job of making us feel insignificant, like a small detail in a cosmic portrait. However, a birthday is much more than that. The day you were born, the universe determined that the world could not exist without you. Whatever higher power you believe in deliberately put you here, and the world was given the gift of you.

You are here to play an indispensable part that only you can play, and that role began the moment you were born. I wholeheartedly believe that the world would be a different place if you did not exist. The people you meet, experiences you have, places you go, and objects you attain will be transformed by your time with them. Even if you don't believe it, you will leave things different from how you found them. We've been conditioned to believe that we are disposable, that our contributions are irrelevant. There is no sense that our life, or anyone else's, is significant to the big picture. Do you believe if you were to go somewhere or make a particular decision, it could fundamentally affect the earth or the people who reside on it?

> **The world would be a different place if you did not exist.**

Ponder that for a moment, and if you don't feel like you make a difference in the world, how passionate can you be toward the things you do and the choices you make? I know you may be thinking, *Well, what if I was never born?* and that's the point. You are inherently significant because you are here, divinely chosen by the cosmos. When you understand that you are absolutely necessary to the story, it changes everything. On your birthday, the whole universe celebrates your existence with a commemoration and an echo of the same energy it invested in you at your genesis. That energy is your life's purpose. I'm not about to claim I know the meaning of life; I don't. Finding your purpose is something you must do alone, but I do know that the first step is consciously creating a space for that possibility. Birthdays are that opportunity. They are a new beginning and a moment of spiritual regeneration. No matter how things were yesterday or last year, you can always try again today.

The
Magick
of
Birthdays

CHAPTER 1

A Walk Through Birthday History

Since the beginning of time, humanity has lifted head and heart heavenward in search of answers to life's questions. Our interest in the sky was the catalyst for three separate subjects: astronomy, astrology, and the calendar. Astronomy is the study of celestial bodies, and astrology posits that the location of those celestial bodies correlates to earthly events. In the early days, there was little to no distinction between these two subjects. The people who were practicing astrology were also practicing astronomy when they first looked to the starry night sky and realized that those far-off shimmering orbs were painting pictures above them.

They observed the changes in the sky and noted patterns in the bodies' rising, setting, shape, and position, which eventually bore the calendar that gave us the ability to celebrate birthdays. A great deal of time has passed since these things were first conceptualized, and to bring us up to the present day, we must journey backward. These subjects originated before recorded human history, which presents a challenge to pinpoint their exact origin. However, historians have used several key events to try to piece together their approximate timelines. We will put ourselves in the shoes of the first skywatchers to understand how these things came to be, which is the first step in utilizing their magic today.

The Prehistoric Era (to 600 BCE)

Welcome to ancient Mesopotamia, circa 2000 BCE, where humankind first recognized these patterns in the sky and developed the earliest calendar. This area is known as a cradle of civilization because it birthed many of the world's first societies. Those early cultures identified the first planets and constellations and developed a rudimentary coded system of astrology. Initially, they used celestial omens to indicate things about large groups of people, such as cities and civilizations as a whole. Called mundane astrology, this simple system says, "if this, then that." For example, they may observe that the crops would flourish when the Moon was in a particular position to Jupiter. Or when Saturn was with Venus, there would be a drought. They compiled their findings for millennia, and that is what built the system we use today.

Then, in around 700 BCE, early astrologists reached a pivotal point in astrological history when they created the zodiac, a virtually unchanged system even today. This made way for natal astrology, a new concept used to make predictions about the lives of individuals. Although it is much simpler than modern versions, the oldest known birth chart dates back to 410 BCE.

Parallel to this, essential developments were happening in Egypt, which also had an astrological system at the time, called Decans. A collection of 36 stars used to mark the progression of hours as they rose over the horizon, Decans are essentially the prototype of what we now know as the 12 houses and were used both calendrically and ceremonially. A fundamental aspect of Egyptian culture was its complex system of polytheistic beliefs and rituals. These practices centered around the pharaoh, who was the divine intermediary between the gods and the Egyptians. A pharaoh's accession to the throne was called a coronation and was completed during several elaborate rites and feasts. When a pharaoh began their reign, they were instantly akin with Horus, god of kingship, who served as guardian of all Egypt. When a pharaoh passed, they would descend to the underworld with Osiris, god of the dead. Scholars believe that this coronation ceremony is the earliest conceptualization of a birthday celebration. Although it did not regard physical birth, Egyptians accepted their pharaohs as gods after they were crowned and, thus, they were reborn.

The Age of Classic Antiquity (600 BCE–476 CE)

ANCIENT GREECE

These concepts eventually traveled to Greece, where the idea of commemorating the birth of a god was expanded upon and significant astrological advances were made through an analytical approach to the heavens. Through a synthesis of the traditions that came before them, the Greeks created Hellenistic astrology. In ancient Greece, astrology was highly regarded as a science and a pillar of religious practices, which were present in all aspects of life. Although numerous gods and goddesses existed in Greek culture, there were 12 significant deities in the Greek pantheon. These were the Olympians, believed to reside on Mount Olympus, each having a specific personality and rule over a particular domain.

One of Greece's most widely venerated deities was and still is Artemis. The daughter of Zeus and sister of Apollo, Artemis is the goddess of wild animals, the hunt, childbirth, chastity, and the Moon. Her most fabled worship site was the Temple of Artemis at Ephesus, one of the Seven Wonders of the Ancient World. Taking over a century to complete, this monumental building was twice the scale of other Greek structures. The temple was said to be fashioned out of marble, adorned with accents of silver and gold, filled with the finest statuary of the age, and completed with an elaborate facade that overlooked a vast courtyard. This is the location where those loyal to Artemis would honor the goddess during the ancient Greek festival of Elaphebolia. They would offer cakes illuminated with candles to symbolize her incandescent beauty and the radiance of the Moon. The candles indicated the signaling of prayer, and blowing them out was a way to lift their messages to Artemis with the rising smoke. Sounds very reminiscent of our modern tradition, doesn't it?

ANCIENT ROME

In our quest to find more answers, we travel across the Mediterranean Sea to the grand city of Rome, where we find Romulus and Remus, twin sons of Mars. As legend has it, these demigods founded Rome on the banks of the Tiber River in 753 BCE. Hellenistic astrology made its way from Greece to Rome, where it was embraced with widespread admiration and credibility. While this fascination with astrology flourished in early Greco-Roman societies, it also began to make its way around the globe, and other cultures began their prophetic study of the stars. Astrology and birthdays became a central feature in Roman culture, and they were the first people to commemorate the birth of nonreligious figures.

At a time when surviving through childhood was an accomplishment, longevity was highly revered. Roman men turning 50 years old were given a special cake baked with wheat flour, olive oil, grated cheese, and honey.

Unfortunately, in their highly patriarchal society, women would not be included until the 12th century, more than 1,100 years later.

Additionally, Romans created holidays to observe the birthdays of their more significant residents, such as emperors. Quite possibly the most renowned engraving from Roman antiquity is the alleged "birthday letter" of Claudia Severa, written to her friend Sulpicia Lepidina around 100 CE. An assistant wrote the beginning of the letter on a wooden tablet in professional penmanship, which dictated the invitation to a formal birthday party on September 11. The last four lines were well wishes, presumably written by Claudia herself.

✳ A NOTE ABOUT GHOSTS ✳

Another critical influence on the future importance of birthdays stems from how these ancient cultures revered the spirit world. It was often thought that you were closer to the spirit world on significant days or ones of major change. Some believed that everyone had a protective spirit present at their birth who was tasked to watch over them throughout their lifetime. By celebrating your birthday, you acknowledge your relationship with this spirit and connection to the other side, which made you particularly susceptible to magic. It's possible that birthday celebrations were used as a form of protection. Guests would offer their best regards—"Happy birthday!" and "Many happy returns of the day!" were traditional greetings. It was believed that good wishes brought good fortune, but the reverse also reigned true, and enemies were to be avoided and only well-wishers invited. The fun and frivolity of these events were not by accident. Music, dancing, and singing were all encouraged to deter any unwanted spirits. Guests would use noisemakers to drive them away and burn candles for protection.

The Middle Ages (476 CE–1450 CE)

Fast forward a few years, and Christianity was steadily gaining traction across Europe, while belief in astrology was diminishing after the fall of the Roman Empire. Early Christians had difficulty accepting the concept of birthdays and considered them an unholy practice, given their ties to pagan gods. The Catholic Church held on to this sentiment for the first few hundred years of its existence but eventually abandoned this way of thinking and began celebrating Christmas as the birth of Jesus. This shift was probably to recruit non-Christian people who were still celebrating the Roman festival of Saturnalia, or the birth of Mithras. Nevertheless, the church slowly became more supportive of the tradition, and birthday celebrations became more widespread. In these Christian societies, only members of the nobility were honored with birthday parties. They did invite commoners to participate, however, reinforcing the social hierarchy in the process. The custom of wearing crowns on birthdays may have originated at these early birthday celebrations.

The Early Modern Era (1450 CE–1750 CE)

After centuries of collecting dust in Greek basements, astrology emerged back into the world. Many notable astronomers and astrologers were born during this time: Giordano Bruno, Tycho Brahe, William Lilly, John Dee, Johannes Kepler, and Galileo Galilei are only a few of these illustrious individuals, and many of their methods are still used today. Scientific developments allowed for more accurate and sophisticated charts to be created, and astrology reached another peak of its power. Astrologers were consulted in every important matter, whether it was choosing a time to go to war, making a medical diagnosis, or advising on the future of a king. Royal families employed court astrologers, and esteemed European universities such as Cambridge held astrology chairs. Astrology was heavily reflected in the art of the time as well as in the literature and architecture.

Meanwhile, the Church had a sneaking suspicion of the power that astrology held and would soon vilify the practice, making it out to be the "devil's work." It was seen as heresy and superstition during the Inquisition, and many astronomers were forced to renounce their astrological beliefs to survive. This, in combination with new scientific discoveries, caused astrology and astronomy to diverge. Sir Isaac Newton made astronomical breakthroughs with his mathematical calculations of the motions of the planets, and a whole new approach to the sky arose.

Rationalism became the most popular consensus in response to the Catholic Church's excessive superstitious authority and control. This new birth of scientific discoveries made way for the Age of Reason. Critical analysis and skepticism were used to reform society and restore balance. Astrology wasn't a crime anymore, but it lost its validity, its connection to both mysticism and science. It was viewed as entertainment, and most astrologers worked under pseudonyms to protect their reputations.

The Modern Era (1750 CE–Present)

An English newspaper article was written for the birth of a member of the royal family, and included within it was an unusual graph: a birth chart. After many years of being regarded as nothing but a parlor trick, astrology once again began to pique people's interest. By now, we are steadily approaching modern day, and birthdays are being celebrated all over the globe. Next stop, 18th-century Germany. Invented by German bakers, Kinderfest was a birthday celebration for children that closely resembles the parties we see today. On a child's birthday, family members awoke them and presented them with gifts and a cake topped with one candle for each year they had been alive, as well as one extra in the hope of living at least one more year—the latter a bit macabre, I'd say.

Unfortunately, during this time birthday cakes were a luxury only the wealthy could afford; commoners could not bear to buy the ingredients needed to make these sugary treats. In fact, we don't find many details about the ordinary person when we look back at history. Only the wealthy had the means to document their lives and important events such as birthdays. Others were not likely to be written about. Many more birthday celebrations could have occurred in the lower classes but just not been documented. I wonder what rich traditions were lost as a result.

During the next period in history, the Industrial Revolution, the required cake ingredients were more widely available, and birthday celebrations flourished regardless of a person's economic status. This, in combination with advances in mass production, allowed bakeries to offer customers ready-made cakes at affordable prices. Through a combination of immigration and a drop in Puritan influence, Americans imported the idea of the German Kinderfest and began hosting children's parties.

At the turn of the 20th century, astrology experienced a major revival in the United States. It was the beginning of modern astrology as we know it today. Until this time, when someone asked you for your sign, they were referring to your rising sign. This changed in the 1930s, when newspapers began writing columns about Sun signs to draw in casual readers, leading to a proliferation of horoscopes based solely on the Sun sign, which is why it's the one everyone knows today. In 1930, astronomers discovered Pluto. Uranus and Neptune had been around for some time, but the discovery of Pluto, as well as newly discovered asteroids, led to a push to integrate these new celestial bodies into the ancient tradition.

For the first time in more than 2,000 years, the fundamental structure of astrology was altered. Innovation overtook tradition, and modern astrologers changed the preestablished planetary scheme of the zodiac. This means that zodiac signs once assigned to traditional planets were adjusted to be ruled by the outer planets Pluto, Uranus, and Neptune. This incorporated new ideas and knowledge our ancestors weren't privy to but unfortunately disregarded a lot of observational data the system was founded upon. This was when modern astrology started to differentiate itself from the traditions that came before. It became heavily influenced by psychology, focused on internal affairs, and was seen as a tool for character analysis rather than something predictive. Nevertheless, this new approach propelled astrology back into the mainstream. It was further popularized by the counterculture movement of the 1960s and then the New Age movement of the 1970s and 1980s.

The last and greatest force of the popularization of astrology has been the development of the personal computer and eventually the internet in 1983. Astrologers who once spent weeks painstakingly creating and interpreting charts with legitimacy that could not be assured could now immediately compute and print out an accurate chart in a matter of minutes. Until this point, you had to know the underlying astronomy and complex mathematics to calculate your natal chart, but now astrology was accessible for anyone who desired to learn.

Since then, technological advances have continued to make leaps and bounds in astrology. For centuries, we couldn't decipher much of the information written by ancient astrologers, but in recent decades, many of these texts have finally been translated into modern languages. In the 1990s, these newly available resources sparked a revival of the ancient traditions as practiced by Babylonian, Hellenistic, Medieval, and Renaissance astrologers. These ancient civilizations may be gone, but the foundation they built lives on. Astrology has overcome many hurdles throughout the centuries yet persists because it is a living tradition that will continue to grow organically alongside humanity for years to come.

Birthdays are much the same; cultures have contributed their customs through generations, evolving them into the celebratory days we see today. We have created folklore and superstition and packed on the magic. I'm sure some of these are coming to mind, like the birthday spankings I mentioned earlier. Honestly, who thought that was a good idea? If only that one would've been lost to time.

Part I

Astrological Magic

CHAPTER 2

What Do the Stars Have in Store for You?

So do the stars really hold the secrets to human destiny? This is the age-old debate of free will versus determinism—and a question that astrology begs the answer to. Free will is the ability to act at one's own discretion without the constraints of necessity or fate. Determinism is the theory and philosophy that all events, including moral choices, are determined by preexisting causes. We may never know if our belief in astrology was merely a baseless superstition or one of humanity's oldest truths, but that does not make it any less valid for the phenomenon that it is.

Astrology has worn many different hats through the years. It's been a way of life, a parlor trick, and even the work of the devil. Funny enough, in all this time arguing over what astrology is, we're still not left with a clear answer, and perhaps that's because it does not belong in any one box. It's not a science, and it's not an art. It's a system of understanding the world around us through the correlation of celestial alignments and earthly events.

I'm often asked, "Does astrology work?" This question has always troubled me. Asking if astrology works is like asking if time works—it just *is*. Many astrologers, including myself, believe that astrology "works" because we live in an interconnected universe and everything within it has an overarching shared experience. Astrology is a mirror. It doesn't make anything happen but reflects reality. It's not causal; there is no bargaining because you are making all the choices. Your birth chart doesn't force you to do anything; rather, you are a certain way, and that is revealed in your chart. So no, it's not a pass to escape moral responsibility.

Astrology is a mirror.

The natal chart is a prewritten autobiography. It is a promise to unfold. It's an illustration of who you are internally and the external circumstances you will experience throughout your lifetime. It is a tool for self-discovery and to assist you in your journey of finding your purpose. The chart is a map of the heavens at the moment of your birth into the world and depicts the precise location of each of the planets. When you interpret your natal chart, you blend the meaning of each planet with the sign and house in which they are located to create an outline of your life.

Your chart is the foundation for most studies you will do within astrology, at least as it relates to you, so before we delve into the material, be sure you have yours. To calculate your chart, you'll need your time, date, and place of birth. I recommend using www.astro.com. It is an excellent resource for anyone looking to become proficient in astrology. This book is framed as both a guide and a workbook, so you will also need a pencil to fill in your personal information as we go through the concepts. There is also a space for notes in the back to write down anything that particularly resonates or prompts your desire for further research.

The Wandering Stars

All the way back in ancient Mesopotamia, when the first star watcher lifted their head to the heavens, this is where astrology began. The heart of astrology is about tracking the "wandering stars" through the sky to watch how they influence your personal aspects and daily transition. Understanding the planets is the first step to reading your natal chart, so we will begin by examining each planet's role and the archetypes behind them. They are like different people, and each works its own job with its own traits, goals, and interests.

This is where we reach our first significant difference between the ancient and modern systems of astrology. Before 1930, when Pluto was discovered, causing the outer planets to be integrated, only seven planets were used within astrology. These are known as the seven traditional planets, and they are the Sun, the Moon, Mercury, Venus, Mars, Jupiter, and Saturn. For thousands of years, these were the only planets known to humankind because they are the only ones observable with the naked eye. It wasn't until the invention of intermediary technology that we could see the outer planets: Uranus, Neptune, and Pluto. There is a fundamental and observational difference between the two groups. This is not to say there is anything wrong with using the outer planets. If you feel called to use them in your practice, you should by all means do so. However, an issue arises when the outer planets take on so much significance that it is to the detriment of the system it was entirely based on.

In the beginning, the planets were called the "wandering stars" because they changed positions, and the stars were called "fixed stars" because they did not. The planets were thought of as messengers who communicated information through their alignments, which we then used to predict what would happen. As seen later in this chapter, for thousands of years, our ancestors would record what the planets were doing and compare it to what was happening to them. The meaning behind the planets is derived from their data compilation.

The planets symbolized the will of the gods and their direct influence over mortal affairs, and the names of the planets have changed over time to reflect the gods in fashion. During the Mesopotamian era, the planets were named after Babylonian gods; around the 6th century BCE, Greek names were used; and eventually they changed to the Roman names we know today. Venus was called Aphrodite by the Greeks, for example, and before that, it was called Ishtar after the Babylonian goddess of love. Today when we speak the names of the planets, we are invoking these divine archetypes. There are also myths associated with each planet. I suggest learning about them because they are rather fascinating and add clarification.

Astrology is not inherently magical, but naturally these two tend to interweave because they are so complementary. When they converge, they create a synthesis called astrological magic, which combines both traditions into something entirely divine. In this chapter you will find a correspondence list for each planet. Let this serve as a foundation to begin building from as we go through the book.

Planets are split into three categories: luminaries, benefics, and malefics. Luminaries are the ones that cast light: the Sun and the Moon. Early astrologers could not differentiate among the different types of celestial bodies and believed the Sun and Moon were planets. Of course, with advances in astronomy, we know this is not accurate, but the verbiage remains the same. For the actual planets, if you look up into the night sky, you'll notice two groups of planets. One group, the benefics, are bright, shiny, and easily visible. The other group, the malefics, appear darker, dusty, and muted. The malefics and benefics are subjective opposites, and their meanings derive from this visible factor. On the next clear night, go outside and try to spot both groups as our predecessors did.

The benefics are called the "doers of good," and they are Venus and Jupiter. The malefics are the "doers of bad," and they are Mars and Saturn. This distinction is an oversimplification of the planets; it's not like if you see Mars in your chart your life is a dumpster fire, or if you see Venus everything's aces. Today these words are polarizing, but the cultures who created this system did not work within a framework of absolute good and absolute bad. They saw a duality present in all of life. Mercury doesn't fit into any of these categories. It becomes whatever the conditions set it out to be. If it is with benefics, it becomes benefic. If it is with malefics, it becomes malefic. It totally would jump off a bridge if all its friends were doing it.

Within the seven traditional planets are five personal planets—the Sun, the Moon, Mercury, Venus, and Mars—and two social planets, Jupiter and Saturn. The personal planets orbit closest to Earth and play a significant role in your individual development. Their placements in your birth chart are indicative of areas you will be heavily drawn to in this lifetime. In contrast, the social planets act as external forces and represent two opposing natures: Jupiter is expansion, and Saturn is withdrawal. As the planets travel around the sky, they visit different zodiac signs. The planets have their preferred signs to visit and other signs they do not particularly enjoy. These planetary vacation spots are called essential dignities, and they determine how well and at what strength the planet expresses itself. If the planets are people, the essential dignity is their mood, which is directly affected by their circumstances.

The Essential Dignities

DOMICILE

When a planet is domicile in a sign, it is relaxing at home. This is the sign over which it has rulership. A planet in domicile will provide smooth sailing.

EXALTATION

When a planet is exalted in a sign, it's an honorary guest in another's home. It's being waited on hand and foot and receives anything it wants very quickly. A planet in exaltation will provide many blessings.

FALL

When a planet is fallen in a sign, it's located directly across from the one it is exalted in. A planet in fall is ignored and struggles to make any real change.

DETRIMENT

When a planet is exiled in a sign, it's located directly opposite from its home. Everything feels out of place here, and they are not suited for the conditions. A planet in detriment will push you out of your comfort zone to grow.

Knowing your essential dignities means taking stock of your chart by accessing your weaknesses and strengths. This is a traditional astrological system that is not particularly common within modern astrology. Although this is just the basics and an oversimplification, understanding your essential dignities can add a lot of depth to how you interpret your chart. As we go through the planets, be on the lookout for significant placements you have within your chart and refer to this list to see what that might mean for you.

The Seven Traditional Planets

THE SUN, KNOWN AS HELIOS |
DIURNAL LUMINARY | MASCULINE

The Sun is the archetype of the celestial god, the dynamic presence and force of being. It rules Leo, it's exalted in Aries, it's fallen in Libra, and it's exiled in Aquarius.

The Sun is a luminary, and it leads the daytime sect of planets. The luminaries light up the galaxy around them and are necessary to see anything. This idea of "sight" tells us a lot about the two luminary planets (the Sun and the Moon). The Sun takes approximately one month to transit across a zodiac sign. Its orbit is always steady, and it is a constant upholding force. It often represents the masculine people of prominence in your life, like fathers. The Sun is located at the center of the solar system and represents the center of ourselves within astrology. Your Sun sign is so much more than your "basic personality." It is your essence, the permanent part deep inside you. Your Sun is what your life is evolving around, and often that is a goal. It is career-based fame. It is what you are known for. It is how you shine. It's who you aspire to be and what you are driven to do through egoic creativity. Embracing your Sun sign will make you feel more fulfilled, provide direction, and give you a sense of purpose.

My Sun sign is _____. It's located in the _____ house.

A full list of correspondences for the Sun is found on pages 91–102.

THE MOON, KNOWN AS SELENE | NOCTURNAL LUMINARY | FEMININE

The Moon is the archetype of the celestial goddess, the emotional force of habit and need. It rules Cancer, it's exalted in Taurus, it's fallen in Scorpio, and it's exiled in Capricorn. The Moon is the second luminary, and it leads the nighttime sect of planets. It has a moist and cool temperament, the conditions for germination. It is a symbol of fertility and femininity and represents the maternal figures in your life. The Moon is the most impermanent of the planets; it is only in a zodiac sign for two and a half days and is constantly waxing and waning through the lunar phases. It represents bodies, cycles, and moods that change; the coming to being; and the passing away of things. It deals with the act of day-by-day travel and what we do to get by. If you've ever immediately regretted doing something and thought to yourself, *Why did I do that?* it was your Moon sign. Your Moon governs your emotional nature, instinctive reactions, and the unconscious habit patterns you have developed through past experiences. When you haven't had the time to think through a situation, your Moon sign responds for you. It is the vulnerable parts of yourself that you keep safe in the shadows. The people who see your Moon at work will be those closest to you. Your Moon sign is how you feel emotionally nurtured and secure, and the way you do that for others.

My Moon sign is _____. It's located in the _____ house.

CORRESPONDENCES OF THE MOON:

Deities: Selene, Hecate, Diana, Artemis, Thoth, Luna (figures associated
  with fertility, clairvoyance, divination, or cycles)

Number: 9

Colors: Silver, white, purple

Tarot card: The Moon

Stones: Moonstone, selenite, labradorite, celestite, pearl, opal,
  aquamarine

Metal: Silver

Flora: Camphor, iris, lettuce, mugwort, waterlily, willow, lavender,
  mullein, poppy, ginger, clary sage, frankincense, myrrh,
  narcissus, mushroom, jasmine, vanilla, ylang ylang, aloe vera

Fauna: Wolf, hare, bat, crab, dolphin

Other: Menstruation, hagstones, melons, ghosts

MERCURY, KNOWN AS HERMES, "THE TWINKLING ONE" | NEUTRAL

Mercury is the archetype of the bestower of intelligence, the mental force of imagination and analysis. It rules both Gemini and Virgo. It's exalted in Virgo, fallen in Pisces, and exiled in Sagittarius. Mercury is the namesake of a Roman deity who served as the messenger to the gods. Within mythology, it is the only planet that can go to both our world and the underworld. It's the ambidextrous figure of the chart. Depending on its placement, it is the only planet that can be on either the day or nighttime team. It is not inherently benefic or malefic, diurnal or nocturnal, or masculine or feminine. Mercury takes 13 to 14 days to transit a zodiac sign and famously goes retrograde three or four times per year. It's the fastest, smallest, and innermost planet with a temperament that varies. Your Mercury sign is your mode of logic, quick-witted intelligence, and intellectual faculties. It is your capacity to collect, sort, and communicate the knowledge you have gained through your life. Mercury is your communication style, the back-and-forth conversation you have with other people. It is the part of you that asks questions and seeks answers. It represents your ability to study, write, and debate. It is how you process information and manage your time and schedule. It deals with transportation and short trips.

My Mercury sign is _____. It's located in the _____ house.

CORRESPONDENCES OF MERCURY:

Deities: Odin, Athena, Anubis, Hermes (messengers and guides, thieves, trid trick\sters, teachers, and magicians)

Number: 8

Colors: Gray, purple, orange

Tarot card: The Magician

Stones: Green moss agate, sodalite, blue lace agate, lapis lazuli, aventurine, lodestone, labradorite

Metals: Aluminum, cinnabar, mercury

Flora: Fennel, lavender, lemon verbena, mandrake, mint, valerian, peppermint, rosemary, eucalyptus, lemongrass, dill, celery, fern

Fauna: Winged animals

Other: Pinkie fingers, feathers

VENUS, KNOWN AS APHRODITE, "THE SPARKLING ONE" | NOCTURNAL | FEMININE

Venus is the archetype of the fertile life force, the magnetism of love and attraction. It rules Taurus and Libra. It's exalted in Pisces, fallen in Virgo, and exiled in Aries and Scorpio. Of all the planets in the sky, Venus is the brightest, most captivating one. It is of the nighttime sect, it's the lesser benefic, and its temperament is moist and hot. Venus takes approximately four or five weeks to transit a zodiac sign and goes retrograde every 18 months. While in retrograde, avoid making significant changes to your appearance. Venus is the planet of pleasure. It represents beauty, love, abundance, art, and feminine figures. Your Venus sign is your attitude toward finances, personal possessions, and how you spend your money. It deals with what is attractive and appealing. It's the type of amusement you are drawn to and the people and things you find valuable. It reflects how you draw yourself to others and others to you, especially romantically or based on your aesthetic values. It is how you express yourself in romantic relationships and reveals your idealized perception of love.

My Venus sign is _____. It's located in the _____ house.

CORRESPONDENCES OF VENUS:

Deities: Freyja, Venus, Aphrodite, Frigg (figures associated with fertility, femininity, sexuality, abundance, relationships, or art)

Number: 7

Colors: Green, pink, red

Tarot card: The Empress

Stones: Rose quartz, rhodonite, unakite, peach moonstone, green aventurine, morganite, emerald, ruby, amethyst, turquoise, malachite, peridot

Metal: Copper

Flora: Catnip, columbine, pennyroyal, periwinkle, vervain, yarrow, rose, geranium, birch, jasmine, sandalwood, lily, eucalyptus, apple, coriander, thyme, benzoin, lilac

Fauna: Sparrow, dove, swan

Other: Coral, sandstone, pearls, saffron, shells, aphrodisiacs

MARS, KNOWN AS ARIES, "THE FIERY ONE" | NOCTURNAL | MASCULINE

Mars is the archetype of the destroyer of life, the motivating force of will and action. It rules Aries and Scorpio. It's exalted in Capricorn, fallen in Cancer, and exiled in Taurus and Libra. Mars is the lesser malefic, of the nighttime sect, and arid and intemperately hot. It takes approximately six or seven weeks to transit a zodiac sign and goes retrograde every two years. During that time, we may have trouble standing up for ourselves and low libido. It's interesting to note that when other planets are retrograde, they take on Martian significations. It's like Mars's infernal rage is applied to them. Mars is the planet of physical energy. It represents athletes, surgeons, soldiers, and metalworkers, as well as siblings and competitors. Mars is eliminatory. It severs things and represents strife, violence, war, robbery, and lying. Named after the god of war himself, Mars certainly lives up to its reputation—it's intense; passionate; and full of raw, unbridled, animalistic instinct. Your Mars sign represents your unleashed energy, the heated passion behind your actions. Your Mars sign is your vitality. It is how you fight, take action, and defend yourself. It governs your sex drive, forcefulness, and aggression.

My Mars sign is _____. It's located in the _____ house.

CORRESPONDENCES OF MARS:

Deities: Ares, Tyr, Mars (warriors)

Number: 5

Color: Red

Tarot card: The Tower

Stones: Carnelian, citrine, fire agate, garnet, ruby, jasper, hematite, pyrite, bloodstone

Metals: Iron, brass

Flora: Galangal, hops, meadow buttercup, tarragon, wormwood, dragon's blood, patchouli, nettle, clove, tobacco, black pepper, basil, garlic, cayenne, cumin, ginger, radish, cacti, thistles, ash

Fauna: Horse, bear, wolf

Other: Used flint, swords, shields, helmets

JUPITER, KNOWN AS ZEUS,
"THE RADIANT ONE" | DIURNAL | MASCULINE

♃

Jupiter is the archetype of the expansive life force. It rules Sagittarius and Pisces. It's exalted in Cancer, fallen in Capricorn, and exiled in Gemini and Virgo. Jupiter is the greater benefic, of the daytime sect, and the largest planet in our solar system. Jupiter takes approximately 12 or 13 months to transit a zodiac sign and goes retrograde once a year, often a time of intellectual development. This colossal giant is hot and moist, the ideal conditions for growth, which can be life-providing or it could consume. Within mythology, Jupiter is the king of the gods, and its regality can be seen in its abundant and intellectual nature. Jupiter's knowledge is on a profound level. It is lived wisdom, gnosis, not just memorizing facts, as opposed to Mercury, which is more data collection. Jupiter governs philosophy, religion, ethics, luck, generosity, prosperity, education, law, and justice. It is teachers, leaders, and gurus. Your Jupiter sign is your search for deeper meaning and truth. The abundant inflation drives you to broaden your horizons; chase your dreams; and expand your mind through education, growth, travel, experiences, opportunities, and spirituality.

My Jupiter sign is _____. It's located in the _____ house.

CORRESPONDENCES OF JUPITER:

Deities: Zeus, Juno, Thor, Isis (figures associated with wind, sky, storms, and fatherhood)

Number: 4

Color: Blue

Tarot card: Wheel of Fortune

Stones: Citrine, lepidolite, amethyst, fluorite, pyrite, turquoise, lapis lazuli,
ammonite, azurite, sodalite, turquoise, sapphire

Metal: Tin

Flora: Agrimony, lime, meadowsweet, oak, pine, sassafras,
thorn apple, saffron, nutmeg, cinnamon, sandalwood,
star anise, honeysuckle, jasmine, copal, hyssop, juniper

Fauna: Eagle, bull

Other: Index fingers, lightning bolts, anything struck by lighting

SATURN, KNOWN AS KRONOS,
"THE SHINING ONE" | NOCTURNAL | MASCULINE

Saturn is the archetype of the boundaries of life, the limiting force of fear and responsibility. This is the last planet we can see with our naked eye, making it an observational boundary of the solar system. It rules Capricorn and Aquarius. It's exalted in Libra, fallen in Aries, and exiled in Leo and Cancer. Saturn is the greater malefic, of the nighttime sect, and dry and frigid, the perfect conditions for death. Saturn takes roughly two and half years to transit a zodiac sign and goes retrograde once a year. During that time, life may feel more restrictive and you'll have to work harder to launch projects. Saturn is connected to the principles of limitation, lessons, punishments, misery, isolation, and the deterioration of your mind and body. It represents the places we go to die, like tombs, coffins, and morgues, but it can also describe things of more significant epochs of time, like administrations, legacies, and dynasties. It is authority figures and people who have gone through something monumental, like orphans, widows, and elders. Your Saturn sign is here to teach you that disciplined hard work will lead to genuinely earned, long-lasting success. It is an insight into the recurring issues you will face until you finally overcome them and emerge as the highest version of yourself.

My Saturn sign is _____. It's located in the _____ house.

You also may be familiar with Saturn in reference to the "Saturnian return," an event that happens nearly every three decades when Saturn reaches the exact point it was the moment when you were born. It's a significant celestial coming-of-age moment or a total existential crisis. It's really the roll of the dice on that one. Depending on how long you live, you could have multiple Saturnian returns within your lifetime; your first occurs around age 29, your second around 59, and your third around 89. They are important transits to be aware of because they often indicate significant lifestyle changes like switching career paths, separating from partners, finding new love, relocating, or making large financial investments. You can calculate them online using a Saturnian return generator.

My first Saturnian return: _____

My second Saturnian return: _____

My third Saturnian return: _____

CORRESPONDENCES OF SATURN:

Deities: Kronos, Bast, Osiris (crones and figures associated with death and lessons)

Number: 3

Color: Black

Tarot card: The World

Stones: Black tourmaline, black kyanite, red jasper, galena, smoky quartz, tiger's-eye, obsidian, onyx, hematite, jet, serpentine

Metal: Lead

Flora: Henbane, monkshood, morning glory, skullcap, patchouli, thyme, elderberry, frankincense, myrrh, cedarwood, valerian root, deadly nightshade, mandrake, pine, hemlock, wolfsbane (Note: many Saturnian plants are poisonous.)

Fauna: Crocodile

Other: Middle fingers, scythes, hourglasses, sulfur

The Outer Planets

The significations of the seven traditional planets display the spectrum of human experience through their contrasting natures. For example, Venus signifies love, unification, and attracting the things we desire, while Mars signifies hatred, separation, and the taking of things we desire. If you look through the planets, you will see this continuous parallel. The Sun emits while the Moon receives, Jupiter is freedom while Saturn is imprisonment, and so forth. The traditional planets are all-encompassing, they are missing nothing, and they can provide you with all the details you could ever need. They are a well-reasoned and long-standing system. Everything is built to complement one another and fits together like corresponding puzzle pieces.

As astronomy becomes more sophisticated and new celestial bodies are discovered, major questions are and will be posed for astrology. Do we include every newly found object in the sky? If so, why? What is the reasoning behind the ones we choose and the ones we don't? This is a long-overdue conversation in the astrological community and one I feel I must touch on. I'm not proposing to toss out the outer planets completely, but I don't recommend using them as sign or house rulers, but instead as energetic qualifiers. I use them as additions, not replacements. They can add further information and insight but in a way that's appropriate and doesn't break the critical foundational structure of astrology. Look at your birth chart and see if Uranus, Neptune, or Pluto are aspecting any of your traditional planets. If they are, think of it like they are influencing that planet with their significations.

URANUS

Uranus indicates spontaneity and incoming change. It represents individuality, innovation, rebellion, and unconventional events.

NEPTUNE

Neptune is associated with mysticism and spiritual awareness. It represents delusions, dreams, imagination, glamours, and healing.

PLUTO

Pluto represents regenerative processes and transformation. It is associated with intensity, psychological turmoil, and power.

The Zodiac Signs

Astrology reflects the sacred rhythms of the earth, and each month the Sun brings a new astrological sign to the forefront. The energy of each zodiac sign is reflected in the time of year it takes place, and it is spiritually intertwined with the human experience. The seasons all have lessons to teach us, and when we view the zodiac signs from a seasonal perspective, we can see how we live out the purpose of each one. In some areas, you are a warm spring breeze. In others, you are a cold winter's night or a crisp autumn rain.

The zodiac is a band of constellations that lies along the Sun's ecliptic. Think of it as a celestial highway that the planets travel through. It is divided into 12 equal zodiac signs, which take up 30° each. The Sun takes one year to travel the zodiac and spends approximately four weeks in each of the zodiac signs. Each sign has its own traits, desires, and way of viewing the world. We all have the same planets in our natal chart, but they express themselves differently based on the constellation in which they are located.

ZODIAC CONSIDERATIONS

The zodiac signs are categorized using four primary considerations: their planetary ruler, modality, triplicity, and polarity. If these words sound like nonsense, don't worry; they make these concepts sound much more complex than they are. The more you familiarize yourself with these ideas and practices, the more they will feel tangible and relevant to your understanding of yourself and others—on your birthday and throughout the year.

PLANETARY RULER

The zodiac signs are the homes of the planets. They do not move; the planets travel through them. The planets are like pictures, and the zodiac is the filter you apply to them. The phrasing is "*X* planet in *Y* sign" because the zodiac signs are not the active part of astrology. Every planet has a home, a zodiac sign in which it is assigned to live. These are called planetary rulers, and they describe where everything ideally belongs. Even the luminaries have homes, but they are the only planets to have just one; the rest of the planets have two.

The Sun: Leo
The Moon: Cancer
Mercury: Gemini and Virgo
Venus: Taurus and Libra
Mars: Aries and Scorpio
Jupiter: Sagittarius and Pisces
Saturn: Capricorn and Aquarius

MODALITY

Modalities are the zodiac signs' qualities; they are also called quadruplicities. The modalities are cardinal, fixed, and mutable, and they repeat in an orderly fashion down the zodiac in that order. Within each modality, there are four signs; they all have the same quality, but different elements rule them. Cardinal signs herald the start of a new season. They are all about initiating ideas, taking action, and making plans. It is not their job to carry things through, only give life to them. The cardinal signs are Aries, Cancer, Libra, and Capricorn. Fixed signs hold down the middle of a season. They are steady, consistent forces that maintain movement. They take the ideas birthed by the cardinal signs and make them a reality. The fixed signs are Taurus, Leo, Scorpio, and Aquarius. Mutable signs rule the transition from one season to the next. They possess effortless fluidity well suited to change and transformation. They are adaptable and think outside the box. The mutable signs are Gemini, Virgo, Sagittarius, and Pisces.

Cardinal: Aries, Cancer, Libra, Capricorn

Fixed: Taurus, Leo, Scorpio, Aquarius

Mutable: Gemini, Virgo, Sagittarius, Pisces

TRIPLICITY

The 12 signs are divided equally into four elements. The elements are fire, earth, air, and water, and they also repeat down the zodiac in that order. Within each triplicity, there are three signs; they all belong to the same element, but they have different qualities. The fire signs (Aries, Leo, and Sagittarius) are passionate, exuberant, temperamental, creative, and adventurous. The earth signs (Taurus, Virgo, and Capricorn) are practical, grounded, sensual, realistic, and loyal. The air signs (Gemini, Libra, and Aquarius) are intellectual, curious, analytical, philosophical, and communicative. The water signs (Cancer, Scorpio, and Pisces) are intuitive, emotional, sensitive, and mysterious.

Fire: Aries, Leo, Sagittarius

Earth: Taurus, Virgo, Capricorn

Air: Gemini, Libra, Aquarius

Water: Cancer, Scorpio, Pisces

POLARITY

Polarity refers to a sign's masculine or feminine nature. This has nothing to do with gender, but rather concerns the energy of the sign itself. The fire and air signs are masculine; they are active and projective. Water and earth signs are feminine; they are receptive and passive.

ARIES | FIRE | CARDINAL | MARCH 21–APRIL 19

There is a newfound lightness in the air that awakens the earth after its long winter rest. Aries is the leading sign of the zodiac and the turbulent initiation of springtime. It is the most abrupt and catalyzing of the signs. It doesn't have the patience to wait for the perfect ice-free day. It pushes forth from under the melting snow. The ground is cold and waterlogged with the spring thaw, and although it is too early to plant, life is beginning to stir. Aries leads us through the vestiges of winter in search of the bright sunny days that lie ahead. To start a fire, you need friction, and Aries is that friction. It is not sustainable fire. It is intemperate and combustible. It is ruled by Mars, which further adds to its incendiary qualities. Aries is hotheaded, which is fitting because within the body, Aries governs the head and is always diving headfirst into situations. Much like it is first in the zodiac, Aries is very competitive and wants to be first in everything. There is a spontaneous urgency to Aries. Its nature is to take action, often without thinking it through beforehand. One of Aries' most beautiful qualities is its pure courage, which is why they are coined "The Hero" of the zodiac.

The Sun enters Aries on the vernal equinox, which marks the beginning of spring. When the Sun transitions through Aries, work spells for authority, rebirth, new life, challenges, courage, new beginnings, protection, and willpower.

CORRESPONDENCES OF ARIES:

Deities: Ares, Amun, Belenus, Ra, Anat, Hestia, Hunga

Colors: Scarlet, orange, white

Tarot card: The Emperor

Stones: Fire agate, garnet, bloodstone, carnelian, citrine, diamond, red jasper, ruby

Metals: Gold, iron, steel

Flora: Alder, cedar, basil, blackberry, peppermint, rosemary, carnation, cinnamon, nettle, ginger, clove, cumin, geranium, gorse, tiger lily, thistle, chestnut, holly

Fauna: Hawk, magpie, robin, woodpecker, ram, tiger, leopard

TAURUS | EARTH | FIXED | APRIL 20–MAY 20

The land is coming alive, and the fields are ripe for planting. Taurus is the gravitas of spring, a time of procreation and celebrating life. The warm rain and wind kiss the rich brown soil, awaken the seeds, and nurture them as they grow, for the germinating seeds of today are the full pantries of tomorrow. Like the roots of a giant oak tree, Taurus grows strong and is sustainable. It is an unwavering force endowed with extreme determination and strength of will. You can depend on Taurus for anything; however, do not hold your breath for them to change because they will hold firm. Tactile senses are fundamental to Taurus, as it is ruled by Venus and longs to be surrounded by love, beauty, and pleasure. Taurus is the "sensualist" of the zodiac, and it governs the neck, an essential body part for sensory awareness. It allows our eyes, nose, and ears to home in on sights, smells, and sounds that give our brain critical information about our surroundings. Taurus is a creature of habit and thrives within structure and stability. They build a habitable world around themselves, and they do not venture too far away from that.

When the Sun transitions through Taurus, work spells for assistance, fertility, growth, careers, family, financial security, healing, health, marriage, material gain, and stability.

CORRESPONDENCES OF TAURUS:

Deities: Aphrodite, Bast, Cernunnos, Dionysus, Horus, Venus, Frigg, Ishtar, Mithras, Isis

Colors: Sapphire, mauve, jade

Tarot cards: The Empress, The Hierophant

Stones: Chrysocolla, emerald, moss agate, diamond, malachite, rose quartz, turquoise

Metals: Brass, copper

Flora: Mandrake, patchouli, apple, hawthorn, magnolia, honeysuckle, raspberry, thyme, vanilla, violet, rose, lily of the valley

Fauna: Cow, beaver, dove, robin, bull, ox

GEMINI | AIR | MUTABLE | MAY 21–JUNE 20

What was green seemingly just a moment before has transformed into a vibrant array of color. From the rain-washed earth, the seeds we planted have blossomed into beautiful flowers, and Gemini is putting on a spectacular show. There is a playfulness to nature in the sky, woodlands, and rivers. Spring is bubbling up to summer, and Gemini carries us through that transition. The feeling of the coming abundance energizes the air. This is a time of discussion and ideas because soon, survival will depend on nature's capacity to adjust to environmental changes. Gemini is ruled by Mercury, which makes it adaptable and flexible to no end but also noncommittal and flaky because it is so unstable. There is an unparalleled duality to Gemini. It is depicted by the twins, and it rules the shoulders to the fingers, the area of the body that changes and splits down the middle. Gemini has a penchant for learning and an incredibly open mind. They are the "brainstormer" of the zodiac, constantly collecting information so they can debate it within themselves. Without intellectual stimulation, Gemini grows restless.

When the Sun transitions through Gemini, work spells for activity, communication, divination, education, imagination, knowledge, luck, neighbors, siblings, success, travel, solving issues, and resolving conflicts.

CORRESPONDENCES OF GEMINI:

Deities: Artemis, Inanna, Seshat, Apollo, Odin, Hermes, Thoth, Freyr
Colors: Light blue, green, white, yellow

Tarot cards: The Lovers, The Magician

Stones: Aquamarine, emerald, alexandrite, fluorite, howlite, lodestone, peridot, citrine

Metal: Mercury

Flora: Beech, chestnut, hazel, hawthorn, bergamot, clover, dill, mugwort, star anise, fennel, marjoram, yarrow, lily of the valley, lavender, eucalyptus

Fauna: Parrot, raven, rooster, deer, horse, butterfly

CANCER | WATER | CARDINAL | JUNE 21–JULY 22

The crops have ripened, and the leaves on the trees are full and emerald green, opening toward the sunlight and breathing in the hot, aromatic air. The heat of the day is exhausting, the kind of weather that invites a deep calm and restfulness. The streams begin to run dry, and the earth yearns for rain to quench the soil. Cancer steps forward as the "nurturer" of the zodiac to tend to all it has created. Cancer is ruled by the Moon, the most maternal of the planets, which also has control over the times. Ironically, in a time when it is the most precious commodity, Cancer is a water sign. They are guided by their emotions and have a reputation for being moody. However, Cancer is only adapting to meet its own needs, much like the Moon goes through phases and the tides change direction. Cancer rules the breasts, an inherently maternal area of the body that supports human life. They care deeply and are very attached to the people closest to them but are guarded to those they are not. Cancer is the crab. It puts up armor around the things it wants to protect. Its defensiveness comes from a place of caring for its home.

The Sun enters Cancer and reaches its peak on the summer solstice. From this day forward, it is once again time to bid farewell to the Sun and anticipate the return of the gentle darkness. When the Sun transitions through Cancer, work spells for comfort, intuition, domestic life, family, gratitude, home, love, prosperity, and protection.

CORRESPONDENCES OF CANCER:

Deities: Ceres, Demeter, Diana, Juno, Mercury

Colors: Blue, silver, yellow

Tarot cards: The Chariot, The High Priestess

Stones: Amber, beryl, calcite, moonstone, selenite, opal, sapphire, pearl, sunstone

Metal: Silver

Flora: Moonflower, catnip, chamomile, lemon balm, water lily, geranium, apple, holly, eucalyptus, milkweed, spruce, jasmine, aloe vera, sandalwood, lotus, algae

Fauna: Beetle, crab, turtle, octopus, dog

LEO | FIRE | FIXED | JULY 23–AUGUST 22

♌

The earth is thriving at its most vibrant peak and celebrating the bounty of the land. Although the air may sometimes feel too hot to breathe, this weather ignites passion and sends Leo's eternal blaze into overdrive. The earth is basking in its success, and Leo takes center stage in a full theatrical spotlight. Leo is ruled by the Sun, which sits at the center of the solar system and illuminates everything around it. Leo behaves in the same way, with both pride and generosity. It wants recognition for its consistency and prowess. In the same way logs must be added to a fire, Leo requires a lot of external support to maintain its constant burn, but it recognizes this and does the same for others. The Sun never goes retrograde, and likewise, Leo is renowned for its stability, loyalty, and consistency. It rules the heart, the animating force of the body, and they fully put their hearts into every relationship and situation they encounter. There is a regality to Leo. They are natural-born leaders bursting with self-confidence, which is why it's the "king" of the zodiac and represented by the lion.

When the Sun transitions through Leo, work spells for confidence, courage, creativity, fame, goals, influence, public speaking, and success.

CORRESPONDENCES OF LEO:

Deities: Hera, Anat, Cybele, Helios, Amun, Hathor, Ra, Sol, Sekhmet

Colors: Gold, orange, yellow, green

Tarot cards: Strength, The Sun

Stones: Amber, garnet, peridot, topaz, tiger's-eye, carnelian, chrysoberyl, labradorite

Metals: Gold, iron

Flora: Cinnamon, eyebright, nutmeg, mistletoe, angelica, heliotrope, sunflower, rue, acacia, chamomile, calamus root, hops, marigold, saffron, cyclamen, frankincense

Fauna: Lion, eagle, peacock, salmon, sturgeon, cougar

VIRGO | EARTH | MUTABLE | AUGUST 23–SEPTEMBER 22

The crops are high in the fields and ready to be harvested, while the brush on the sides of the road is left scorched by the summer Sun, which is now finally drawing to a close. Virgo is the transition from the heat of summer into autumn and the preparation that must be done to survive the dark winter ahead. Virgo is the "maiden" of the zodiac, depicted as the virgin holding the wheat branch. It is not related to sexuality but in reference to crops needing to be processed before they are edible. It deals with what needs to be broken down and determines what to keep and what to discard. Virgo is doing this in every aspect of life, which is why it rules the digestive system. It systematically plans and makes decisions for both the present and future. Virgo takes a careful approach and uses logical explanations. Virgo's reflective analysis is a gift from Mercury, its ruling planet, which grants it a great attention to detail. However, Virgo can become hypercritical in their hopes of reaching perfection. Virgo has a deep sense of humanity and wants to share their information with others. They are always there to help, lend an ear, or give advice.

When the Sun transitions through Virgo, work spells for clarity, communication, details, employment, financial planning, foundations, healing, organization, paperwork, precision, and research.

CORRESPONDENCES OF VIRGO:

Deities: Anat, Artemis, Demeter, Persephone, Odin, Hestia, Diana, Isis, Heru, Adonis

Colors: Brown, gray, navy blue, purple

Tarot cards: The Hermit, The Magician

Stones: Amazonite, amethyst, andalusite, apatite, sardonyx, chrysocolla, charoite

Metal: Mercury

Flora: Beech, maple, oak, dill, aster, lavender, patchouli, valerian, hyacinth, marjoram, cornflower, elder, lily, narcissus, rosemary, cypress, moss, peppermint

Fauna: Bear, cat, pig, squirrel, magpie

LIBRA | AIR | CARDINAL | SEPTEMBER 23–OCTOBER 22

A cool breeze carries summer away. Flower petals begin to curl and brown, and leaves fall like confetti on the sidewalks. The crops have all been harvested, and there is no more work to do in the fields. The earth is now resting, regenerating. We are halfway between the searing hot days of summer and the frigidly cold days of winter. Libra arrives as a garland of scarlet and gold to teach us to work in balance with nature, like leaves blending in harmonious autumnal hues. Libra is the "diplomat" of the zodiac. It makes decisions and facilitates discussions that will carry us safely through the winter. It is passionate about justice, law, and legal matters. It is represented by the scales and rules the stabilizing middle ground of the body, the hips. Even when it isn't looking for exact balance, it weighs things and discriminates between factors. Its intellectual curiosity is boundless, and it wants to investigate all perspectives. Debating, relating, and conversing with others is very important to Libra. It is ruled by the planet Venus, which drives it to seek harmony and gives it an eye for beauty.

The Sun enters Libra on the autumnal equinox and marks the beginning of fall.

When the Sun transitions through Libra, work spells for balance, creativity, expression, justice, legal matters, new love, new projects, partnerships, and truth.

CORRESPONDENCES OF LIBRA:

Deities: Aphrodite, Athena, Frigg, Astraea, Hephaestus, Venus, Minerva, Mithras

Colors: Royal blue, green, violet, gray

Tarot cards: The Empress, Justice

Stones: Ametrine, desert rose, lepidolite, kyanite, diamond, smoky quartz, marble

Metal: Copper

Flora: Cherry, witch hazel, foxglove, lilac, spearmint, strawberry, belladonna, mullein, thyme, catnip, marjoram, sweet pea

Fauna: Dove, goose, sparrow, hare, snake

SCORPIO | WATER | FIXED | OCTOBER 23–NOVEMBER 21

The temperature grows colder with each passing day as the earth descends into darkness. Earth's more delicate creations begin to die, and the elements take a significant toll on those strong enough to survive. The foliage that was new and green only months ago will soon fall to the earth to decompose, and it is from this death that new life will regenerate in the spring. This profoundly transformational period is Scorpio, and it lives in this never-ending metamorphosis of death and rebirth. Its transmutable qualities lend it to be the "alchemist" of the zodiac. It has a deep awareness of the spectrum of human experience. It is highly intuitive and fascinated by the occult. It rules the genitals and reproductive organs, the area of the body that allows creation. It is represented by the scorpion, an animal exceptionally well equipped for battle with a penetrating lethal weapon. Scorpio lies in wait, collecting information, and it is always one step ahead. They are cunning, manipulative, and act out when feeling vulnerable. It is ruled by Mars, which further empowers it to dominate situations and people. Scorpio is truly magnetic.

When the Sun transitions through Scorpio, work spells for emotional problems, inner work, ancestors, psychic abilities, protection, banishing, transformation, and secrets.

CORRESPONDENCES OF SCORPIO:

Deities: Anubis, Hecate, Hel, Persephone, Ereshkigal, Njord

Colors: Black, navy, crimson, brown

Tarot card: Death

Stones: Alexandrite, beryl, bloodstone, jasper, obsidian, rhodochrosite, ruby, jet

Metals: Copper, iron, steel

Flora: Chrysanthemum, heather, pomegranate, ash, gardenia, allspice, myrrh, nettle, thistle, black thorn, horseradish, nightshade, tobacco, wormwood, elder, cattail, benzoin

Fauna: Vulture, snake, panther, wolf, scorpion

SAGITTARIUS | FIRE | MUTABLE | NOVEMBER 22–DECEMBER 21

Autumn is fading out like a softly sung hymn. Most of the day is washed in sable brown, stormy gray, and finally midnight black. Night arrives sooner each day and lingers long into the morning, when frost begins to coat the ground. Survival now depends on foresight and vision. The wind stings, and the frigid cold brings the warmth out of Sagittarius. Known as the "adventurer" of the zodiac, they are represented by a mythological creature, the archer centaur. They are half-man, half-beast, a combination of animalistic instinct and human intellect. It rules the glutes and legs, the solid and sturdy powerhouse of the body. They seek out a questlike experience of life fueled by wanderlust. Their explorative spirit takes them around the world in search of deeper meanings. Jupiter rules Sagittarius, so their enthusiasm knows no bounds. Their daydreams are an all-encompassing forest fire. Sagittarius is always searching for something they're missing, which leads them to never be satisfied.

When the Sun transitions through Sagittarius, work spells for business success, cooperation, expanding, growth, healing, inspiration, mediation, publishing, removing obstacles, and travel.

CORRESPONDENCES OF SAGITTARIUS:

Deities: Anat, Rhiannon, Diana, Artemis, Hades, Thor
Colors: Brown, gold, purple, maroon
Tarot cards: Temperance, Wheel of Fortune

Stones: Amber, amethyst, zircon, lolite, sodalite, azurite, smoky quartz,
  labradorite

Metal: Tin

Flora: Cedar, rowan, aster, Saint John's wort, star anise, frankincense,
  ginger, carnation, cinnamon, garden sage,
  wallflower, mulberry, chestnut, juniper

Fauna: Elk, horse, lion, monkey

CAPRICORN | EARTH | CARDINAL | DECEMBER 22–JANUARY 19

The newly fallen snow sparkles and crunches like sugar underfoot. It may be winter, but it is beautiful. A deep cold settles across the earth. The land looks desolate as life above and below has gone into hibernation. Life lies dormant in the branches within each barren tree, for Capricorn knows it is time to go within and wait. Ruled by Saturn, Capricorn thrives in this environment strictly outlined by rules and regulations because nature must stall to survive. They govern the bones, the structure that holds our body together. Capricorn is represented by the sea goat, another mythological creature equipped for traversing mountainous terrain and navigating the depths of the oceans. They tread carefully and scope out their environment before proceeding. Everything they do contributes to their utmost success. They are steady, self-disciplined, focused on their plan, and go step by step to achieve that dream, which is why they are the "wise elder" of the zodiac. They are motivated by building their magnum opus and actualizing their dreams into reality. They are incredibly dependable but often impose their own rules on others and become overbearing.

The Sun enters Capricorn on the winter solstice and marks the beginning of winter. On this day the Sun stops its decline and, for a few days, rises in nearly the same spot. Then, like magic, the Sun starts to go north again, and the light returns to our world. While the Sun transitions through Capricorn, work spells for ambitions, banishing debt, boundaries, elimination, foundations, health, organization, structure, and endurance.

CORRESPONDENCES OF CAPRICORN:

Deities: Aphrodite, Freya, Gaia, Hecate, Juno, Agni, Baal, Dionysus, Freyr, Pan

Colors: Black, dark green, indigo, maroon

Tarot card: The Devil

Stones: Black diamond, azurite, bloodstone, malachite, obsidian, onyx, jet, hematite

Metals: Lead, silver

Flora: Spruce, elm, cypress, elder, cinnamon, patchouli, rue, woodruff, vervain, carnation, musk

Fauna: Snow goose, heron, owl, dolphin, elephant, goat, dog

AQUARIUS | AIR | FIXED | JANUARY 20–FEBRUARY 18

Now is the coldest time of the year, but there is a freshness in the air of midwinter. Deep below the surface of the frozen earth, the roots are beginning to prepare for new life. The weather does not permit for anything practical to be done. Instead, it is time to discuss ideas, plan for the future, and devise inventions. During the darkest point of the year, light comes from Aquarius. Right now, everything in nature is self-sufficient, it fends for itself, and Aquarius is this individuality. This is where it gets its out-of-the-box thinking, the potency for delivering radical, grounded ideas. It focuses on what came before to use as a foundation for what is yet to come. It is known as the "humanitarian" of the zodiac, represented by the water bearer because it has a deliverer-of-life essence. Aquarius rules the ankles, which support them to connect to the earth and stand for everyone. They are ruled by Saturn because Aquarius takes us into the next calendar year and challenges its boundaries.

When the Sun transitions through Aquarius, work spells for clarity, friendships, inspiration, invention, advancement, social events, problem-solving, and the greater good.

CORRESPONDENCES OF AQUARIUS:

Deities: Ea, Astarte, Ishtar, Isis, Juno, Nut, Ganymede

Colors: Silver, violet, mint

Tarot card: The Star

Stones: Angelite, aquamarine, aventurine, fluorite, opal, turquoise, amethyst, lapis lazuli

Metals: Aluminum, lead, silver

Flora: Olive, dandelion, patchouli, bittersweet, foxglove, acacia, violet, frankincense, aspen, almond, peppermint, lavender

Fauna: Cuckoo, peacock, albatross, otter, sheep, eagle

PISCES | WATER | MUTABLE | FEBRUARY 19–MARCH 20

The soft, loamy earth is damp with the spring thaw. The days feel warmer, although you can still see your breath rise to the sky as warm vapor. Moisture is so abundant you can feel it in the air. The rivers appear still, but under their blanket of ice, they are flowing free. The days are lengthening as the temperature starts to rise alongside the feelings of hope and optimism Pisces has for the future. The earth is in a state of limbo, for the Sun has made its way through through each of the zodiac signs. The cycle has completed, but has not yet begun again. This is represented in the image of Pisces, two fish swimming in opposite directions, indicative of its ability to see the truth from every point of view. It is known as the "mystic" because it has learned the lessons of the signs that came before it to make it the most empathic of the zodiac. Pisces is ruled by Jupiter, which continuously expands its emotional intelligence and drives it to explore connections and shared experiences with others. Pisces governs the feet, reminding them to stay grounded in the material world and not become enveloped by their emotions. This adaptable sign guides us into a new cycle with its intuitive understanding of the natural order and ultimately shows us that life continues.

When the Sun transitions through Pisces, work spells for art, creativity, cleansing, dreams, psychic abilities, and reconnecting with your spiritual path.

CORRESPONDENCES OF PISCES:

Deities: Sedna, Aegir, Cupid, Eros, Poseidon, Diana, Vishnu
Colors: Aqua, lavender, white, pink

Tarot cards: The Hanged Man, The Moon

Stones: Alexandrite, blue lace agate, staurolite, sugilite, moonstone, aquamarine

Metals: Silver, tin

Flora: Willow, cypress, hyacinth, lovage, reed, garden sage, jasmine, gardenia, sandalwood, carnation, chicory, heliotrope, parsley, poppy, primrose, catnip, iris

Fauna: Ox, horse, sheep, seal, stork, swan, fish

✳ A NOTE ABOUT THE SOUTHERN HEMISPHERE ✳

Our earth has two hemispheres, and they experience the seasons and days opposite to one another. If it is the summer solstice in one while it is the winter solstice in the other, does astrology still work? Yes, because this is a symbolic system. Aries is a new beginning, regardless of whether it marks the beginning of physical spring.

Zodiac Season Spell

If there's one period of the year in which every zodiac sign thrives, it's their solar season, the month-long period when they are aligned with the Sun. Your zodiac season is your moment in the spotlight. It's a vibrant energy that lights you from within and empowers you to be uniquely yourself. Usually, the time of year people tend to adore most is their birth month because whether they know it or not, this is a momentous time of personal power. Not only can zodiac seasons affect your Sun sign as the Sun travels through the zodiac, but they also shine a light on the area of your life ruled by that specific sign. During Aries season, you'll feel a need to begin new ventures wherever Aries falls in your chart, and during Libra season, you'll do the same but seek balance. It's important to note that in the month before your zodiac season, the Sun is located in your 12th house of isolation. Plan to spend some time in the shadows in that time before your zodiac season so you can truly shine on your solar return. This is a customizable ritual to welcome in your zodiac season as you approach your solar return and all the blessings it has to offer.

TIMING:

+ To be done on the first day of your zodiac season

MATERIALS:

+ A pillar candle in a color associated with your zodiac sign
+ Firesafe plate
+ Olive oil
+ A dried herb, plant, or flower associated with your zodiac sign
+ Knife or sewing needle
+ Match

The location of this ritual is essential. Choose a location that connects you to the element of your Sun sign. This doesn't have to be extravagant, but it should be personal to you and somewhere quiet, where you are comfortable and will not be disturbed. If you are a fire sign, perhaps look for somewhere bright and sunny or next to a fireplace. If you are a water sign, try to sit by a river or even use your bathtub. If you are an air sign, look for a high elevation or just an open window. If you are an earth sign, venture to the forest or lie in the grass.

After scouting a proper location, face the direction that your element rules and set up your area for spellwork. (Air is east, fire is south, water is west, and earth is north.) Cleanse yourself, your space, and your tools. If you would like to cast a circle, this is the moment to do so. Get into a comfortable position, close your eyes, and hold your candle laced between your fingers. To begin, take 12 deep breaths, one for each zodiac sign. Breathe in, hold your lungs full, exhale, and hold your lungs empty for a count of three. Breathwork is a very helpful tool to reach a meditative state. When you are there, think about your element and visualize its physical manifestation and characteristics in as many senses as possible. If you are a fire sign, perhaps it's a bonfire; listen to the logs snapping and crackling in the heat, smell the smoke, watch the golden sparks rise into the night sky, and feel the warmth on your cheeks. Channel this energy into the candle in your hands. Stay here in your element for a few moments, whether it is a fire, a foggy forest floor, a vibrant coral reef, or translucent, pearly clouds.

When you feel completely energized by your element, shift your awareness back into your conscious self. Pick up the knife or needle, and engrave the symbol of your zodiac sign into the candle. Then place a small drop of oil in your palm to anoint the candle. Begin with the top and work your way to the base of the candle. This is to symbolize drawing energy inward. Hold the candle horizontally, and lightly sprinkle it with some of the plant, again starting at the top and working your way to the bottom. Place the candle onto the plate in front of you, light it with a match, and say:

I carry this elemental energy into the zodiac season ahead of me,
brightening my path with guiding light

to greet my solar return with all my might.
By the powers of fire, earth, wind, and sea, as I speak it so it be.

Stay in this moment for as long you desire and then mindfully snuff out your candle and close the circle if needed. This candle is intended to be created on the day the Sun moves into your zodiac sign and then remain on your altar for the entirety of the season. Light this candle at least once a day to prepare for your solar return and intentionally create a space of meditation and mindfulness. You can incorporate this candle into other workings, fire scry with it, or just leave it burning while you journal.

The Twelve Houses

The houses form the framework of your birth chart. Unlike the planets and zodiac signs, the houses are not energies or archetypes. Instead, they give context about the landscape of your life that the planets and signs will influence, where their power is destined to present itself. The houses ground astrology in earthly matters because each is assigned to a specific area of life. They describe things both internally and externally out in the world. The first six are "personal houses" because they govern aspects of daily life, and the last six are "interpersonal houses" that concern your connection to the world around you. Every birth chart has 12 houses in it, and all the topics for each house are the same. However, it is your unique combination of planets and signs that fall in these houses that color the story of your life. Every planet in your birth chart is located in a sign and a house, so the phrasing is "I have X planet, in Y sign, in Z house."

HOUSE TYPES

Just as the zodiac signs are divided into groups based on their qualities, the houses are, too. There are three types of houses: angular, succedent, and cadent. These add an important dimension to be aware of while you are interpreting your chart.

ANGULAR | 1ST, 4TH, 7TH, AND 10TH

Angular houses have the most profound impact on the chart. They are the building blocks of you and reflect your actions in the present moment. The planets located in these houses are the most visible in your chart and contain life's most pertinent questions: "Who am I?" "Where did I come from?" and "Where am I going?" They reflect basic human needs through the self, relationships, home life, and career.

SUCCEDENT | 2ND, 5TH, 8TH, AND 11TH

Succedent houses follow angular, in both sequence and impact. They are influenced by both you and the environment around you and rule important life matters such as finances, relationships, love, and death. They represent stability, material foundations, willpower, and sense of purpose.

CADENT | 3RD, 6TH, 9TH, AND 12TH

Cadent houses have the least influence over the chart and rule secondary issues and matters outside of your control, such as friends, obligations, illness, travel, and isolation. They are associated with activity and communication. They are the contemplation before action.

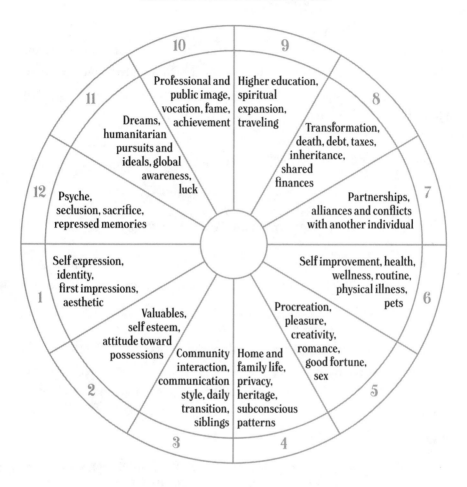

**1ST HOUSE | HOUSE OF SELF | ANGULAR |
RULED BY ARIES AND MARS**

This is the sign that was rising over the horizon the moment you were born. It is where the sky met the earth and your spirit entered your body. This is your ascendent, your most fundamental house. This is the intermediary of your mind and body, your vitality, and it comprises your identity as a whole. It is your initial demeanor and physical appearance, the persona you radiate, and the image you project to others. It shows you take initiative and begin new things. The placements in this house are very relevant to your identity, and the planet that rules your ascendant is your chart ruler.

The planet that rules my chart is _____.

2ND HOUSE | HOUSE OF VALUES | SUCCEDENT | RULED BY TAURUS AND VENUS

This house reveals your concept of value and how you provide for yourself. It is your relationship toward finances, possessions, and resources. Oftentimes it is referred to as your "cash sector." However, it is much deeper than that. It is your image of self-worth and how well you provide for yourself as a result. These are not just monetary values, but how you nourish yourself. It is the things that make you feel secure and supported. The placements here reveal how you spend and hold on to valuables and cherish your belongings. They can also indicate issues of greed, low self-esteem, and financial hardship.

3RD HOUSE | HOUSE OF SHARING | CADENT | RULED BY GEMINI AND MERCURY

This house is your community-based affairs, and it revolves around the people and places you interact with on a daily basis. Placements here are indicative of your normal routine and how you express yourself in your immediate environment. It rules siblings, classmates, neighbors, coworkers, friends, teachers, early education, libraries, and social media. It is comfortable short-term travel, like your daily commute. This house is naturally ruled by Mercury, so this is the area of your chart that will become messy while it's in retrograde.

4TH HOUSE | HOUSE OF HOME AND FAMILY | ANGULAR | RULED BY CANCER AND THE MOON

This is the darkest, most private part of the chart. This is midnight, and it is below the earth. This house sits at the very bottom of the chart. It is the foundation for all things. These are your roots. It represents parental background, ancestry, home, and early life. Placements here reveal what makes you feel safe, how private you are, and the physical home environment you need and will create for yourself. This is your sense of home, both the physical place you live and the people who bring you comfort. It is things you inherit from your family, like property, emotional patterns, experiences, and memories. The fourth house also rules ancestors.

5TH HOUSE | HOUSE OF PLEASURE | SUCCEDENT | RULED BY LEO AND THE SUN

This house encompasses the activities you do because you enjoy them and the things you bring into the world. It relates to children, romance, sex, fun, and creativity. It is what you bring into existence by way of your creation, which can be via reproduction or a legacy. It can be anything you create that takes on a life of its own. Your natural creativity manifests in this area. It is your self-expression, drama, recreational hobbies, and activities you enjoy. It is how you spend your free time.

6TH HOUSE | HOUSE OF HEALTH | CADENT | RULED BY VIRGO AND MERCURY

To do the things you *want* to do, there are things you *have* to do. This house is the chores that keep you functioning, the obstacles you must overcome to show up physically in the world. This is not your career, but the unsung work and service you put in to get there. Placements here will influence your attitude toward everyday duties and requirements. This is your work ethic and wellness because it dictates how physically capable you are of doing the labor. It relates to all aspects of a healthy lifestyle like your diet, nutrition, exercise, and the quest for self-improvement. Pets, employees, and subordinates all show up here as well for the role they play in our daily responsibilities.

7TH HOUSE | HOUSE OF BALANCE | ANGULAR | RULED BY LIBRA AND VENUS

This house is our intimate relationships with other people, the one-to-one bonds we have. This is all partnerships—professional, personal, and romantic. This is your interaction with the person directly across the table from you, which could be a lover, business partner, competitor, or enemy. Legal matters also show here, as well contracts and other agreements between two parties. Your placements here reveal how you treat and relate to other individuals and the type of person you tend to attract in these dynamics.

8TH HOUSE | HOUSE OF TRANSFORMATION | SUCCEDENT | RULED BY SCORPIO AND MARS

This is the house of death. It rules endings and the subsequent new beginnings they inevitably bring. This is metamorphosis, decay, funeral homes, cemeteries, loss, grief, and clairvoyance. This house is buried, which means its contents are hidden and are difficult to see and self-actualize. In turn, it is associated with secrets and the taboo. This house is all about the natural exchange of energy and the things you get from other people, like money, inheritances, alimony, debts, loans, and psychological baggage. Placements here can indicate an interest in the occult or a life of tumultuous death, as in you will experience the death of others many times. It reveals your feelings toward your own mortality and could also indicate that you help other people through their deeper issues, like as a therapist or counselor.

9TH HOUSE | HOUSE OF PURPOSE | CADENT | RULED BY SAGITTARIUS AND JUPITER

This house is the path of knowledge. It relates to all aspects of personal evolution. It pertains to broadening your mind and your horizons. It's a journey both mentally and physically. It represents the complex matters the mind is driven to explore, like philosophy, law, politics, higher education, belief systems, religion, and different cultures and languages. It can be foreign and multicultural affairs, international traveling, publishing, broadcasting, and the departure from ordinary life. Placements here indicate a lifelong pursuit of knowledge, development of personal belief, and becoming wise in a certain lineage.

10TH HOUSE | HOUSE OF ENTERPRISE | ANGULAR | RULED BY CAPRICORN AND SATURN

This house is the highest ecliptic point. This is your midheaven. This is the most visible portion of the sky. It is high noon, and it is the same part of you. This is your reputation, your public image. It is what you are known for. As you go through your life, this is the part of you that you carefully curate. It takes conscious work and effort to build this pursuit. It is honors, achievements, fame, tradition, and discipline. If you are seeking clarity on your career, this is where you want to look.

11TH HOUSE | HOUSE OF BLESSINGS | SUCCEDENT | RULED BY AQUARIUS AND SATURN

This house is the social collective that supports you and the goodness that is out of your control. This represents the audience that supports you, the groups and organizations you are a part of that believe in the same things you do. Oftentimes celebrities have really loaded 11th houses because these are not close, interpersonal relationships, but rather the society around you as a whole. It is technological advances, dreams, collective goals, and aspirations for the betterment of humanity. Placements here indicate your relationship with socializing and your role within a community.

12TH HOUSE | HOUSE OF SACRIFICE | CADENT | RULED BY PISCES AND JUPITER

This is darkness before dawn. This is the house of endings and the deepest evolution of our soul. This is the sign you were in when your mother was giving birth to you. It is otherworldly. It is between realities. It represents separation from society, the subconscious mind, mysteries, betrayal, spiritual growth through isolation, hidden agendas, and enemies. It is the places we go to be alone and lose ourselves, and it is the parts of ourselves we do not know exist. It is hospitals, prisons, mental institutions, and our inner world of self-sabotage. If you have placements here, you may assist others in these very challenging positions, or it may reveal how you spend your time in isolation.

The planets I have in my 1st house are _____.

The planets I have in my 2nd house are _____.

The planets I have in my 3rd house are _____.

The planets I have in my 4th house are _____.

The planets I have in my 5th house are _____.

The planets I have in my 6th house are _____.

The planets I have in my 7th house are _____.

The planets I have in my 8th house are _____.

The planets I have in my 9th house are _____.

The planets I have in my 10th house are _____.

The planets I have in my 11th house are _____.

The planets I have in my 12th house are _____.

Aspects

Okay, so Mercury is conjunct Venus, but what does that actually mean? As the planets move through the signs and houses, they send messages to one another when they link at certain mathematical angles. These angles are called planetary aspects, and they are the conversations the planets have with one another.

Are they seeing eye to eye, enjoying the company, and working as a team, or are they antagonizing each other and creating problems for you?

This is the part of astrology where people tend to back off because aspects look like convoluted equations, which can be overwhelming for beginners. Unfortunately, if you read a chart without aspects, you're only getting half of the information. I understand the hesitation; I'm comically bad at math, and I don't want anyone to feel discouraged. Rest assured, aspects are total frauds. They only look complicated. We will break them down piece by piece in a way that's as uncomplicated as possible.

Each planet constantly sends out seven rays: one opposition, two trines, two squares, and two sextiles. When they hit another planet, that is when the aspect happens, when there is a recipient. The planets emit their rays to an entire zodiac sign, but the closer that ray is by degree to another planet, the more intense the aspect is.

Aspects fall into "good" and "bad" categories the same way the benefics and malefics do. There are beneficial aspects, trines and sextiles, and more difficult ones, squares and oppositions. All the aspects are by degrees: a sextile occurs when two planets are around 60° apart, a square is 90°, a trine is 120°, and an opposition is 180°.

OPPOSITION

When planets are directly across the chart from one another, they form an opposition. They're separated by five zodiac signs, or 180°. They're in conflict. There's a rivalry between them, an antagonism. There is a battle to be held, and one of them will win and suppress the other.

SQUARE

When planets are separated by two zodiac signs, or 90°, they form a square. This is a state of constant friction and irritation. These planets are on the brink of something adversarial, like they are squaring up to fight. Contrary to what you may think, this is not always bad. They are producing heat and tension, and sometimes that is necessary or even helpful. This highlights action and shows that work is required to reap your desired outcome.

TRINE

When planets are separated by three signs, or 120°, they form a trine. This always takes place in zodiac signs of the same element. Trines are the most powerfully positive out of the bunch. These planets do not get in each other's way but instead share a mutual understanding. Their energy is harmonious and flows with ease.

SEXTILE

When planets are separated by one sign, or 60°, they form a sextile. These planets have a soft and comfortable relationship, but they are not in a hurry to bring you blessings. Your action is heavily required to activate their energy and the opportunities they provide.

CONJUNCTION

When two planets are sitting right next to one another, they form a conjunction. When planets are conjunct, they are melding their energies together. If loving planet Venus was really conjunct with communicative planet Mercury, they would blend their powers and assist you in having a productive conversation with your love interest or opening up about your feelings and attraction to that individual. Conjunction is not technically an aspect because these planets do not hit each other with their rays.

Weaving the Story

We have identified the essential components of the birth chart, planets, zodiac signs, houses, and aspects. These are the pieces you need to weave together the story of the chart. Now that we have built a foundation and know what we're looking for, what does it mean? Let's go back to the beginning and work our way step by step through the process of reading a chart.

Starting with the planets, let's identify if you have a day or night chart. Find where your Sun is placed on your birth chart. If it is above the ascendant-descendant line, you have a daytime chart. If your Sun falls below, you have a nighttime chart. The way the planets act in your chart will depend on whether they fall within that sect or if they are contrary to that sect. When a planet is not where it wants to be, the more troublesome it becomes. Mars is the lesser malefic, and it is nocturnal. If you have a daytime chart, Mars will wreak more havoc than it would if you had a nighttime chart. Mars is grumpier in a day chart because it is out of sect. Your Moon sign may be considerably more important than your Sun sign if you have a night chart. The Moon takes on more significance in a night chart because it is the leader of the sect and what was lighting up the sky when you were born.

I have a _____ chart.

Next, check how comfortable your planets are within your signs. Are they located in their home sign, or are they exalted, exiled, or fallen?

The Sun is _____.

The Moon is _____.

Mercury is _____.

Venus is _____.

Mars is _____.

Jupiter is _____.

Saturn is _____.

Notice the balance of your chart. Do you have many planets concentrated in one area? If you have three or more located in a single sign or house, that is called a stellium. This is a significant area in your life and something you should nurture, especially if these are personal planets, or better yet, a luminary. Do you have an absence of planets in another? Empty signs and houses do not indicate you will never experience those things; they are just not a major focus and there are fewer contributing factors in that area.

I have a stellium in _____. The planets are

_____.

Pay special attention to your angular houses. The planets located there have the most viability in the chart. Examine the relationships between the planets, and notice their challenging and supportive aspects. The information this leads you to uncover will propel you in the right direction to be able to lean on your strengths and improve your weaknesses. Astrology is a never-ending stream of knowledge, and there is always more to uncover. May the tools in this book implore you to dive deeper within yourself and gain a greater understanding of the impact and power your birth chart holds.

CHAPTER 3

The Moon

O f all the celestial bodies, the Moon garners special attention. She's always played a critical role in the lives of people around the globe, but today an ever-increasing crowd is connecting with her as part of their spiritual practice.

Seemingly out of nowhere, there were countless articles about full Moon rituals, and the lunar phases were plastered on everything. It's become so sensationalized that it might feel like a trend. However, I don't believe that. We are intrinsically connected to the Moon and, for one reason or another, have always lived in sync with her cycles. She tells farmers when to plant and harvest, creates tides for fishermen, and guides travelers through the dark.

Nature was once an inseparable part of our lives, but somewhere along the way, we lost our connection. We paved concrete over wild places and turned them into cities, creating such a divide between us and the natural world that it feels like an object. We see ourselves as separate from nature, like we are entitled to have domain over it as if it only exists to serve human needs. Today most of the population lives in urban areas and spends a majority of their days indoors. They do not rely on the ecosystem around them but rather industrialized processes to meet their daily needs. Their lives are devoid of frogs croaking, brooks babbling, and the damp forest air that feels like you are breathing for the first time with each inhale. They are disconnected from the natural cycles and seasons of the earth. Copious amounts of research are showing that our disconnection with nature has an adverse impact on our mental and physical health.

The rising interest in the Moon is not a coincidence but a hunger to return to how things used to be. Living by the lunar cycles is a natural way to foster a connection with nature. We are profoundly influenced by the Moon. Many believe its gravitational pull draws out emotions, affects sleep, and influences menstrual cycles. Although this is difficult to prove, the sheer number of people who believe there is a connection between human behavior and the Moon is undeniable. When you discover truth in the cycles of nature, it makes you realize that you are affected by far more than what is going on internally, and that is a natural segue into magic.

New Moon

This is the beginning of the lunar cycle and the best time for new endeavors. The Moon is missing from the sky; it is a blank slate. Try to complete all past projects by the new Moon so you can initiate new ones at this time. This is the phase to plant metaphorical seeds because the intentions you set now will grow with the Moon as it waxes. Center your spellwork around this theme of growth and the things you wish to create, receive, and manifest in this new cycle. Meditate on these things, and create a list of actions to take in the mundane world to further these magical intentions. This is an ideal time to set up a new altar or begin a new spiritual practice.

From our perspective on Earth, the new Moon occurs when the Sun and Moon align. This means if you were born during this time, your Sun and Moon signs are the same. This is a fortunate birthday to have because you are in tune with your wants and needs. Your head and heart are in perfect harmony. You are not troubled with inner conflict. Your spirit craves beginnings. You enjoy trying new places, activities, and people. You are overflowing with an abundance of new ideas, and there is a childlike curiosity to you, a wonder. You are keen to take action and even a little bit reactive. Others have trouble keeping up with your pace, vitality, and enthusiasm. Although you may strike like a match, you were born when the Moon was weakest, and you have difficulty sustaining energy. You often find yourself abandoning projects when you find the next best thing.

Waxing Moon

This is the two-week period approaching the full Moon. The Moon is swelling and gaining strength. In the same way, the lunar cycle is building. This is the phase to focus on increasing things of your own. You established your desires during the new Moon, and now it is time to take practical steps to bring them to fruition. Center your spellwork around this theme of expanding and boosting output. This is an excellent opportunity for prosperity and fertility workings, gaining knowledge, developing relationships, and facilitating communication of all types, personal or professional.

If you were born during the waxing Moon, you excel at fostering relationships and new skills. You are passionate and decisive with the focus to see things through. You were born when the Moon was about to reach its peak, and in turn, you always feel as if you are on the cusp of something great. You face a never-ending struggle to feel fulfilled because you are hypercritical; nothing feels good enough. Your spirit is detail-oriented. You have a gift for improvement and identifying problems before they become more significant issues. You keep a calm head and provide an anchor for others in times of crisis, especially emergencies. You are nurturing and push others to reach new heights in their lives. People born during this phase are often consultants, advisers, or therapists. However, not everyone is ready to hear your advice, so be mindful not to overstep.

Full Moon

The Moon has reached its peak. This is the most dynamic phase of the lunar cycle. Everything has accumulated up to this moment, and the seeds you planted have blossomed. This is a celebration, a time of fulfillment, basking under the bright light of the Moon in all her majesty. This illumination sheds light on situations that were previously hidden. This is a time for truth spells and getting the recognition you deserve. Center your spellwork around this theme of completion. This is an excellent opportunity to charge things under the light of the full Moon, whether that be crystals, tools, jewelry, or yourself. Channel this uplifting energy for self-improvement and to bring blessings to yourself and loved ones. The full Moon brings increased psychic awareness, making it a good time for divination and spirit work.

The full Moon occurs when the Moon is located directly opposite the Sun. This means if you were born during this time, your Sun and Moon signs oppose one another. This is a challenging birthday to have because you are conflicted between what is logical and what your heart wants. You have conflicting desires pulling you in all directions. Your unpredictability is exhilarating, but you are inconsistent and indecisive.

The Moon was at its apex at your birth, and it instilled in you a hunger for a full life.

You possess a powerful, luminous presence, and others cannot help but be intrigued. Your mystique stems from your internal conflict because you naturally understand opposition. You're great with others.

Waning Moon

This is the two-week period following the full Moon. Its strength is diminishing, and soon it will meld into the velvet black sky. Utilize this period as a catalyst to remove stagnant and unwanted energy and release the things holding you back. Center your spellwork around this theme of elimination. Break your bad habits, and shed unwanted relationships and patterns. Use this opportunity to cleanse, banish, and declutter your space. Alongside the Moon, dive into your darkness. Introspect and have difficult conversations with yourself. Delegate time to reset before the upcoming lunar cycle, and give thanks for the things that manifested during the previous one.

If you were born during the waning Moon, you were imprinted with a sense of learned wisdom. You're the quintessential "old soul." A quality about you •
feels frozen in time. Moving on is challenging because you are so deeply sentimental. You tend to stay in relationships and situations you have outgrown. Material success does not satisfy you; rather, you seek fulfillment through service to others. People born during this phase are often teachers, entertainers, and storytellers because they are nostalgic and embed their knowledge with others.

I was born under a _____ Moon.

* MAGICAL DAYS OF THE WEEK *

With all this attention on the Moon, it may surprise you to know that it is only a small aspect of a larger system called planetary timing. In the same way we follow the lunar phases, there are other cycles we can incorporate into our spells and rituals. Each of the seven traditional planets rules over a different day of the week, giving them varying energies, strengths, and weaknesses we can use in our favor. Each day takes on the significations of the planet that rules it, as does the individual born on that specific day. Whichever day of the week you were born on is a day of personal power that you should use to your advantage. Which celestial body are you a child of?

Which celestial body are you a child of?

SUNDAY, RULED BY THE SUN

Sunday is an uplifting and joyous day. Use this energy to start a new venture, make something known, or launch a new project. Enjoy lighthearted hobbies, relax, and rejuvenate. Focus on self-expression and creative endeavors. This is a great day to work with god energy and tap into your divine masculine.

- Try spells related to healing, confidence, agriculture, creativity, spirituality, personal growth, beginning anew, masculinity, and solar power.

Children of the Sun are the luckiest. They are believed to be vibrant and creative but self-centered. They are natural-born leaders and have a positive outlook on life.

MONDAY, RULED BY THE MOON

Monday is the most restful day. Listen to the needs of your body and mind, and use this energy for reconnection to yourself. Practice self-care, journal, or do restorative movements like stretching or slow flow yoga. Don't overexert yourself or engage in strenuous activities. Tasks should revolve around nurturing yourself, like meal prepping for the week ahead, planning your grocery list, reading, or spending time in nature. This is a great day to work with goddess energy and tap into your divine feminine.

- Try spells related to the home, cleansing, peace, dreams, healing, femininity, fertility, glamours, intuition, psychic ability, and lunar power.

Children of the Moon are the most beautiful. They are believed to be intuitive and romantic but overly sensitive. They experience a lot of instability throughout their life but will find comfort in home and family.

TUESDAY, RULED BY MARS

Tuesday is the most intense day. Utilize this energy to move forward, make decisions, and get things done. Prioritize your weightiest tasks for today. Whether they are physically or mentally demanding, you will find the motivation to push through. This is an ideal time to exercise, challenge your limits, and face conflict head-on. Channel your Martian energy to set boundaries, sever toxic relationships, and stand your ground.

- Try spells related to passion, victory, dominance, warding, physical and emotional strength, courage, sexuality, cord cutting, and return-to-senders.

Children of Mars are the most ambitious. They are believed to be courageous and enthusiastic but impatient. They have such a drive to be successful that they might destroy things in their wake.

WEDNESDAY, RULED BY MERCURY

Wednesday is for critical thinking and honest self-expression. Communication will be your strong suit today, so schedule important events like public speaking and interviews. Focus on the professional aspects of your life, make business-related decisions, work on marketing, and coordinate activities or events. This is a good time for social interaction, networking, engaging online, or just spending time with family and friends.

- Try spells related to knowledge, charisma, communication, popularity, and adaptability.

Children of Mercury are the most eloquent. They are believed to be logical and versatile but unreliable. They are brilliant but spend most of their time overthinking things.

THURSDAY, RULED BY JUPITER

Thursday is for abundance in all areas of life. This is the time to stimulate your mind and challenge yourself to expand your horizons in every sense. Take a class, learn a new skill, reconnect to your spirituality, meditate, or travel. Luck is on your side today, so play the lottery and speak to people of authority—ask your boss for a promotion or your professor for extra credit.

- Try spells related to abundance, growth, luck, money, generosity, travel, and storms.

Children of Jupiter are the most philosophical. They are believed to be generous and honest but overbearing. They are optimistic to the point of blind optimism.

FRIDAY, RULED BY VENUS

Friday is for appreciating the finer things in life. Tap into your Venetian spirit and spoil yourself, get a massage, go to the spa, or get your hair done. This is the day to indulge and be frivolous. Go shopping—not for the things you *need*, but the things you *want*. Dress in the way you feel the most beautiful, and get your photo taken. Be more affectionate and empathetic with yourself and your loved ones. The magnetism of this day brings things together, so it's a great time to join a new group and put yourself out there.

- Try spells related to love, romance, wealth, glamours, beauty, self-love, fertility, harmony, friendship, and reconciliation.

Children of Venus are the most artistic. They are believed to be peaceful and creative but self-absorbed. They curate a life surrounded by beauty but are dependent on the opinions of others and are motivated to impress them.

SATURDAY, RULED BY SATURN

Saturday is a day of structure and saying no. Take a pause from making decisions, and step away from business matters. If possible, this is an excellent time to take the day off, to set a boundary against working, to reset. Reflect on the past week because it's time for anything that no longer serves you to pack its bags. Do whatever you need to begin anew on Sunday.

- Try spells related to cleansing, banishment, release, warding, protection, or longevity.

Children of Saturn are the most resilient. They are believed to be resourceful and practical but harsh. They are born into a challenging life but are equipped to overcome and persevere.

Planetary timing is like swimming with the current instead of against it. When you understand these attributes, you can utilize them to amplify the intentions you're putting out into the universe and even plan your schedule around the planetary timing that best supports it. This can be as simple or complex as you choose, and within any spell, you can use multiple layers of planetary timing to create the perfect combination. The deeper you delve into astrology, the more you can incorporate it into your practice.

This is helpful in deciding when to begin your rituals and complete them. If it is long-term working like a money bowl, you could tend to it each Thursday with Jupiter's abundant energy to keep the momentum going. You could cast a banishing spell during a waning Moon on a Saturday. You can also aspect them together. If you wanted to do a spell for boosting communication in a romantic relationship, you could do it during a waxing Moon on a Wednesday. If you wish to be even more specific with your timing, each of these planetary days can be further broken down into 24 planetary hours. This requires a bit of math, but luckily, calculators are available online to use if you so choose.

CHAPTER 4

The Sun

Our universe is brimming with billions of stars, but it is the brightest star at the center of it all that we depend on most. The Sun holds immense power and influence over our Earth, for if there were no Sun, there would be no life on our planet. Without it, there would be no warmth, light, or gravitational pull keeping the planets on their paths. The Sun creates the seasons; each year, we have a cold winter, where the Sun dims, the nights get longer, and the days get shorter. Then the Sun is reborn, and the earth awakens in springtime. There is an abundance of life sprouting with our Sun approaching its peak, summer. Then the warm Earth begins to cool as it approaches autumn, eventually descending into hibernation, and winter begins again.

This annual cycle is produced through the relationship between the earth and the Sun. When observed from our moving planet, the Sun's path appears to revolve around the earth. (Although of course the opposite is true.) The sun's movement determines the changing of seasons on this path, called the ecliptic.

This is the foundation for the tropical zodiac and the calendar. For example, the autumnal equinox occurs each year when the earth crosses the celestial equator, which is our equator extended out into space. When the Sun reaches the celestial equator on the ecliptic, it is the first day of autumn and the beginning of Libra season. The zodiac seasons are particularly important for those whose birthday falls within that month. Your season is a time of great astrological strength because it contains the rarest, most significant solar event of the year, and it happens just for you.

Your Solar Return

Each birthday you have a solar return. This means that the Sun reaches the exact degree it was when you were born. Every year it cycles back to this location, as it has been doing for millions of years. Theoretically, at birth you were imprinted with the energy of the celestial bodies' positions. Much like crystals are tuned to a particular frequency, your being instinctively aligned with the first energies it met in that specific moment and location. These energies are your life's purpose, and they are ingrained in you for as long as you live. At the moment of your solar return each year, you begin to resonate and align again with these original frequencies. Your solar return activates an upward spiral of energy for you to tap into. If you choose to engage with it, this can be a potent time for you and your craft. Working magic on your birthday takes advantage of both your personal power and the alignment of solar energy. It is a way to deliberately welcome what you want to manifest in the upcoming cycle. Despite this event taking place only once a year, you can continue this momentum of solar energy by working in sync with it. This will give your practice an entirely new dimension. The Sun has been celebrated in many forms by different cultures around the world, and here I hope to guide you in your journey of incorporating the Sun into your magical practice.

My solar return is _____.

Solar Return Birthday Ritual

Here's a yearly ritual to welcome in your solar return and realign with your life's purpose on your birthday. This is a time to renew your connection with the Sun and illuminate all roads of opportunity for the coming year.

MATERIALS:

- Solar Return Oil (recipe follows)
- Bowl
- Raw honey
- Rolled oats
- Ground cinnamon
- Gold glitter
- Yellow pillar candle
- Firesafe plate
- Matches or lighter
- A coin that is significant to you, minted in the year or location you were born
- Tweezers

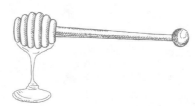

This ritual is to be done with a clear, unobstructed view of the Sun. Choose a location that feels refreshing, like an open door of possibilities. Hopefully, choose somewhere in nature where you will not be disturbed, but if that's not possible, try to find a spot inside near an open window. Settle into a comfortable position on the ground, and lay all your materials out in front of you. Rest your hands palms up on your lap, and surrender your weight to the earth below you. With your eyes closed, tilt your head heavenward and feel the warm rays of the Sun shining down upon you. Let it flow like honey down your body, starting at your head, melting down your arms into your legs and back into the earth. Take three deep breaths, holding for a moment between each. Visualize radiant solar energy entering your being with each inhalation, and imagine the light purifying you, your workspace, and your tools with each exhalation. This is an excellent method to cleanse before any solar working.

The ritual begins with the creation of the Solar Return Oil, which is what you'll be using to anoint the candle. This oil is your solar return encapsulated. It is sunshine in a bottle and shines brilliantly on all levels of happiness.

Solar Return Oil

For external use only.

MATERIALS:

- Funnel
- 2-ounce dropper bottle
- Just under 2 ounces sunflower oil to use as a carrier
- 5 drops lemon oil
- 5 drops orange oil

- 3 drops frankincense oil
- Pinch of chamomile

Use the funnel to fill the bottle nearly to the top with sunflower oil and then add each of the other ingredients. As you add them the bottle, inhale the aromas and say *"Imbue, infuse, impart"* three times as you envision solar energy melding into the ingredients. Seal the bottle, and swirl to mix well.

Add a dime-sized amount of the Solar Return Oil to the bowl followed by a drop of honey, a dash of oats, and a sprinkle of cinnamon and glitter. Honey is sticky and sweet; it represents all the positive energies and opportunities you wish to stick to you. It is crafted by worker bees, and by way of its properties, you invite the help of the worker bees of the universe to intervene in your favor; these powers, however, you see or call them. Oats symbolize abundance and prosperity. Cinnamon, ruled by the Sun and associated with the fire element, boosts power, wellness, passion, and confidence. Gold glitter reminds us of the Sun's indecent beauty, and the candle's yellow color symbolizes imagination, creativity, good fortune, and bright invitations. In combination, all of this weaves a powerful solar return ritual and sets up a year of great potential.

Using your ring finger, which is ruled by the Sun, stir the ingredients clockwise to blend them. As you do, allow your mind to daydream about the year to come. Imagine a door opening in front of you; you cannot see where it leads, but it is blindingly bright with possibility. Spend a moment here in wonderland and then pour the enchanted mixture into the palm of your hand. Warm it up between your fingers, and anoint the candle while you speak this incantation: *"An elixir mixed to obtain what I require, through anointing this candle I secure what I desire."* Begin at the top of the candle and work your way to the base to symbolize the lure to your life of all things positive. Set the candle on the plate, and light the wick. Lift your hands to the Sun and say, *"O glorious Sun shining down upon me today, I honor you on my solar return for all the blessings that may. I open the door; I turn the chapter; I trust in you for what's to come after. Bring me stability, prosperity, laughter. This is my greatest year yet, and it cannot come faster."*

Now with the coin, you will create a talisman, an object that has been imbued with specific energy through ritual that is then either carried or kept in a location to attract energy or protect it within that space. In this case, it will hold the power of your solar return. Use the tweezers to pick up the coin and pass it through the candle flame three times while saying, *"Solar return candle, I call upon you. By glow of your flame, charge and infuse; this coin shall be your muse."* Pause for a moment and feel yourself full of bliss. Allow your dreams to foam up to the surface and pop like champagne bubbles into the world around you. Immediately journal about your experience today so that you can look back at it a year from now on your next solar return. The candle should be brought to your altar to burn out and then used in a carromancy reading. Be sure to save the remains for future use.

Solar Altars

It's essential to have a place in the physical world where you feel comfortable to practice your craft. An altar is just that—a sacred space to conduct your workings, ground yourself, meditate, store your tools, honor your deities or ancestors, and connect to the divine. An altar is a very personal thing. Depending on the culture or tradition you belong to, it will look different from person to person. There are many kinds of altars, and some are dedicated to specific types of practices. Perhaps someone who worships Aphrodite would have a beauty altar in their bathroom, adorned with seashells and pastel colors. Another person who works heavily with kitchen magic may have an enchanted pantry full of herbs and vegetables and a spoon they use as a wand. You are going to create an altar to honor yourself and your solar return.

Find the place in your house or bedroom that has the best natural lighting, someplace warm and inviting, where you can feel the Sun's rays shining down on you. This is the perfect location to set up your altar. However, if this isn't compatible with your situation, or you already have an altar, that's perfectly fine. These are only ideas to inspire you and elements you may want to incorporate into your practice. If you are in the broom closet (those of you practicing witchcraft in secret), you can build your altar in a box or something equally discreet that you can easily hide.

We created three items during the Solar Return Birthday Ritual to begin building our altar: the solar return wax remains, oil, and talisman. These are our first tools to start working with the Sun and continue the momentum of our solar return throughout the year. They are the gateway to reconnect to that moment in time, and coming up, you will find several spells that utilize them as ingredients. As the book progresses, you will craft more tools for your altar and continue to use the ones you have in a practical way. As for other items you can use to decorate the altar, look to the correspondences of the Sun, listed later in the chapter, for ideas and inspiration.

Solar Return Chart

Your solar return chart is the story of the next year of your life. It has a plot, setting, new characters, and a twist or two. It's calculated using the exact moment the Sun returns to its natal position, the location it was when you were born. This chart depicts the planetary transits that occur during the 12 months from one birthday to the next and is an excellent tool to assess and predict the themes that will arise.

The location used for the chart is not the place an individual was born, but instead where they are at the moment of their solar return that year. Depending on where you are located on your birthday, you will have a completely different chart. Some may use this in their favor by strategically traveling to a place that sets them up for a year of astrological strength.

A solar return chart is read much like a natal chart, but it is for a shorter duration of time. Each birthday, you can cast a chart for the year ahead and use the tools in this book to decipher it. The planetary locations reveal the areas of prominent activity, while their aspects are the support and conflicts of interest. The most important component of the chart is the placement of the Sun. It's the overarching theme of the story, the central idea of the year ahead. This is a forecast for the Sun in each of the 12 houses to easily get a glance at what's to come.

Sun in the Solar Return

1ST HOUSE

If the Sun is located in the 1st house, this is a year of individual action and personal success. It's a time to focus on yourself and discover new skills, talents, and capabilities you didn't even know you possessed. Begin new projects, especially those that contribute to your life goals, or return to a passion you left in the past. Your self-image will go through a transformation, and your outward appearance will change. You will receive recognition for something you've put out into the world, which could be related to the development of your career or identity.

2ND HOUSE

If the Sun is located in the 2nd house, this is a prosperous year centered around earning potential and understanding the value of stability. You are focused on bringing security to your material world, balancing finances, getting out of debt, and making investments. You will be compensated for the difficult work you have accomplished through monetary gain. This year you will be saving for an important purchase or making one.

3RD HOUSE

If the Sun is located in the 3rd house, this is a year of mental stimulation and deviation from your normal routine. Your mind is motivated to consume as much information as possible. You may begin a new educational pursuit or travel on many short trips. Your daily commute will change. Perhaps you will begin working in a new setting or purchase a new vehicle. Strange events in your sphere will rise and cause you to become more involved with your community, family, neighbors, or colleagues.

4TH HOUSE

If the Sun is located in the 4th house, this is a year to strengthen your internal foundation and deepen your connection to those who bring you emotional comfort. Developments will be made in your family dynamic. Possibly a member will vacate, a baby will be born, or you will adopt a new pet. Your home may change through relocation or renovation. You will find yourself diving into your roots, your heritage, and your ancestral lineage, possibly through venerating your ancestors in your practice. You may feel the desire to create something from the ground up.

5TH HOUSE

If the Sun is located in the 5th house, this is a year of honest self-expression and following your heart. You will find yourself diving into projects and engaging in activities that feel like play to reignite your passions. This is a busy year spent exploring new places, activities, and lifestyles; eating out; and attending public events. You will actively create things, whether that be new relationships, interests, or even children.

6TH HOUSE

If the Sun is located in the 6th house, personal health and routine will be brought into focus this year. You are diligent in maintaining a healthier lifestyle through exercise and proper nutrition. You increase your productivity by becoming regimented and detailed. The conscious effort you are applying causes your daily routine to shift and relieves stress from your mind, body, and spirit. Your place of work and relationships with coworkers may change.

7TH HOUSE

If the Sun is located in the 7th house, this year is centered around the interpersonal relationships you care the most about. The bonds you share with others will transform. You may see a new serious relationship or a development in an existing one. This is not reserved for romantic partners. You could also find yourself partnering up at work, signing contracts, and making agreements.

8TH HOUSE

If the Sun is located in the 8th house, this is a year of deep exploration within the self. It's a time of introspection to heal yourself from the inside out, to figure out who you are and how to utilize that person out in the world. The theme of this year is metamorphosis. You may experience the loss of a loved one or see the end of a significant chapter in your life. The power of others is reflected in your finances, investments, and inheritances. You could find yourself owing others or others owing you in some capacity.

9TH HOUSE

If the Sun is located in the 9th house, this is a year of broadening your mind. The beliefs that frame your reality will evolve as you seek out more profound experiences. This could be the result of traveling abroad, exploring different philosophies and spiritual beliefs, or pursuing higher education. You will do this in an extroverted way, opening up opportunities to meet wise individuals in your specific field of interest that will help guide you during this time.

10TH HOUSE

If the Sun is located in the 10th house, this year's prominence will be brought to your career and public persona. You will be more attuned with what others expect from you and emphasize success and achievement. This is a high point of some aspect of your life. You are hitting your stride and polishing your future. Your reputation among people of power will greatly improve, leading you to receive accolades, honors, and promotions.

11TH HOUSE

If the Sun is located in the 11th house, your plans will be realized and your dreams will be turned into practice. You will embrace your individuality while becoming more active in causes you believe in and joining groups based on wanting to be part of something bigger than yourself. You will connect with others passionate about the same subjects as you, which often manifests as charitable work and other humanitarian pursuits.

12TH HOUSE

If the Sun is located in the 12th house, this year will be turned inward to prepare for a new cycle. This is a time of rest and reprieve. You will undergo significant spiritual development in healthy solitude. You are coming to terms with the past, facing the music, and releasing old baggage. You must hide away to heal what is necessary and be able to create from a place of depth.

✴ PERSONAL YEAR NUMBER ✴

In combination with where your Sun is located in your solar return chart, you can also check to see which personal year you are entering. Within numerology, the personal year cycle is a nine-year rotation that we repeatedly cycle through our entire lives. Each year is assigned its own themes. This is the calculation to find out yours—and like your solar return chart, it's a way to divine your future for the year that lies ahead.

HOW TO CALCULATE YOUR PERSONAL YEAR NUMBER

- Add the digits of your birthday and the current year. If your birthday is September 1 and the current year is 2022, the digits are 9, 1, 2, 0, 2, 2.
- The sum of those digits is $9 + 1 + 2 + 0 + 2 + 2 = 16$.
- Add the digits of the sum, repeating until you get a single number.
- 16 consists of two digits (1 and 6), making the final total $1 + 6 = 7$.
- This person is in year 7 of their personal year cycle, and on their next birthday, they will enter their 8th year.

Blend the meaning of your personal year number with the placement of your Sun in your solar return chart to divine clarity on the next year of your life.

YEAR 1

This is the beginning of the cycle. You are entering into a new chapter of life. Although it may be unfamiliar, know that the universe is supporting you to stand on your own. Year 1 is all about independence and personal achievement. If anything is holding you back, now is the time to shed that unwanted energy so you may initiate new ventures to the fullest.

YEAR 2

After a few turbulent years full of change, you are ready to slow down and plant roots. Year 2 focuses on nurturing yourself and your relationships, developing patience, and determining what you need to feel secure.

YEAR 3

Now that you are feeling more stable, this is the time for self-discovery. Year 3 is for following your creativity and seeking self-improvement. Last year you discovered what you need out of life; this year you discover what you want. This is a fun year, a time to travel, learn a new skill, explore a new lifestyle, or sport a new look. In your quest for improvement, you may outgrow relationships.

YEAR 4

After exploring your options the preceding year and deciding what you're after, now you have a clear vision to execute your plans. Year 4 is a time to methodically plan your goals and the steps you must take to build the life of your dreams. You will put in the hard work and establish a stable foundation for a career, family, relationships, and health.

YEAR 5

You have begun to build something, and you are navigating uncharted waters. Year 5 is all about adaptability and embracing uncertainty. The year is bustling and filled with ups and downs, but change is exciting when you learn to roll with the punches. Embrace new opportunities, and you will grow in ways you could have never imagined.

YEAR 6

Your connections to other people are called into question, and this forces you to evaluate your interpersonal relationships. This includes romantic partnerships, friendships, and colleagues. In the 6th year, a major decision may be made regarding another individual.

YEAR 7

After thoroughly evaluating your surroundings over the past few years, it is time to journey inward. The 7th year tests your faith and implores you to explore your inner world. This is a time of introspection, pursuing developments in your spiritual practice, and gathering higher knowledge.

YEAR 8

The profound spiritual growth you experienced the preceding year has granted newfound empowerment. The 8th year is all about stepping into your personal power and making the most of your life. There is a focus on financial well-being, assets, and personal property.

YEAR 9

This is the end of the cycle. You are closing the door on this chapter of your life. It is a time for completing tasks, tying up loose ends, and making space for change. You could be relocating, switching jobs, or changing partners. The 9th year is your phoenix moment. The mythological bird knows when it's time to destroy its nest and engulf itself in flames, only to be reborn from the ashes. Now it's your turn.

Correspondences of the Sun

When you hear the word *Sun*, what feelings does it bring about? Do you envision yourself sitting in the grass on a warm summer's day, the Sun gently beaming down on you, warming you from overhead? Perhaps you imagine a winter's day so cold that only the Sun's reflection off the snow makes it bearable to venture outside. Or you may recall a nasty sunburn, one so awful it made your skin peel and even the air hurt your skin. The emotions this exercise is evoking are your personal correspondences, your own symbolic magical links. This is the place you draw energy from to power your spellwork. It is a tool to focus your intention.

I have written multiple magical correspondences lists within this book, including the one you are about to read. They are based in history, folklore, mythology, and medicine, but they are ultimately highly personal to the individual. There's no point in choosing the "right" color, herb, crystal, or Moon phase in a spell when you do not understand the significance of why you are using them. The information provided within these pages is meant to inspire you, not limit you. If I have written a spell that does not resonate with you or a correspondence you disagree with, change it. Follow your intuition. It is your compass.

Follow your intuition. It is your compass.

Symbolism is a vehicle for deeper understanding. It allows us to convey energy that lays beyond what words can describe. This is a general list of themes and correspondences associated with the Sun, along with their individual magical properties. Use this as inspiration for your spellwork, journal prompts, grimoire pages, divination, and altar décor.

THEMES:

Abundance, business, change, charisma, clairvoyance, clarity, cleansing, coincidence, comfort, confidence, courage, creativity, destruction, ego, enthusiasm, fame, fertility, friendship, gratitude, growth, happiness, health, hope, illumination, justice, leadership, light, luck, passion, positivity, productivity, prosperity, protection, risk, sexuality, strength, success, truth, vitality, warmth, wealth

PLANTS:

> **Angelica:** Acceptance, binding, banishment, hex breaking, harmony, dreams, visions
>
> **Bay leaf:** Blessings, courage, fame, prosperity, wish granting, banishment, release
>
> **Cactus:** Protection, longevity, determination, willpower, warding, chastity, banishment
>
> **Galangal:** Banishment, hatred, reversal, justice, sympathy, protection, wealth, desire
>
> **Ginseng:** Activation, attraction, endurance, spirits, longevity, fertility, memory, negativity
>
> **Goldenseal:** Beauty, business, growth, healing, money, prosperity, strength, wisdom
>
> **Lovage:** Attraction, dreams, passion, romance, sex, negativity, purification, renewal
>
> **Mistletoe:** Activation, banishment, beauty, rebirth, love, home life, prosperity, sexuality
>
> **Rosemary:** Purification, protection, hex breaking, heartbreak, luck, memory, love

FLOWERS:

Black-eyed Susan: Shadow work, release, suppressed emotion, trauma, cord cutting

Buttercup: Abundance, divination, protection, psychic abilities, engagement, inner child

Calendula: Stability, strength, legal matters, growth, prophetic dreams, protection, luck

Carnation: Beauty, truth, justice, love, fertility, protection, consecration, vitality, strength

Celandine: Happiness, protection, release, escape, legal matters, breaking patterns

Chamomile: Calm, dreams, nightmares, wealth, visions, introspection, creativity, luck

Chrysanthemum: Innocence, love, ward off unwanted spirits, protection, mysteries

Daffodil: The afterlife, faeries, beauty, calm, friendship, nightmares, new beginnings

Daisy: Attraction, blessings, challenges, lust, youth, skills, healing, purpose, divination

Dandelion: Wishes, animal protection, divination, happiness, cleansing, summoning

Daylily: Forgetfulness, easing sorrow and pain, femininity, devotion, sacrifice, struggle

Eyebright: Clairvoyance, clarity, divination, dreams, visions, insight, memory, skill, truth

Goldenrod: Issues, beauty, challenges, divination, loss, luck, wealth, finding treasure

Heliotrope: Banishment, courage, healing, wealth, devotion, finding lost objects, sleep

Hibiscus: Divination, love, attraction, liberation, passion, independence, spiritual growth

Lotus: The afterlife, attachment, consecration, dreams, purification, generosity, wisdom

Marigold: Affection, the afterlife, transformation, consecration, dedication, happiness

Marshmallow: Protection, cleansing, psychic abilities, healing, love, fertility, grieving

Morning glory: Divination, astral travel, psychic abilities, divine guidance, clarity, calm

Peony: Banishment, anger, uncovering secrets, release, luck, protection, preserving

Poppy: The afterlife, funerals, assertiveness, challenges, visions, wealth, hatred, lust

Rue: Protection, health, healing, purification, balance, clarity, hex breaking, warding

Saint John's wort: Protection of animals, banishment, security, justice, courage, spirits

Sunflower: Wish granting, clarity, fertility, self-confidence, happiness, obstacles, wealth

Witch hazel: Banishment, healing, loss, protection, wisdom, beauty, amplifying magic

TREES:

Acacia: Divination, clairvoyance, psychic ability, consecration, the afterlife, wisdom

Ash: Ambition, concentration, communication, creativity, protection, strength, travel

Birch: Banishment, security, determination, sleep, lunar magic, beginnings, protection

Cedar: Confidence, comfort, wealth, introspection, luck, spell reversal, protection

Hazel: Fertility, wish granting, love, protection, wisdom, divination, healing, inspiration

Juniper: Protection from theft, banishment, hex breaking, secrets, dreams, cleansing

Oak: Abundance, the afterlife, authority, consecration, endurance, motivation, fertility

Pine: Abundance, perseverance, longevity, fertility, memory, purification, protection

Rowan: Family, faeries, divination, forgiveness, grounding, broadening perspectives

RESINS:

Benzoin: Prosperity, purification, energizing, banishing, upliftment, prosperity, focus

Copal: Purification, love, protection, grounding, centering, creating a sacred space

Frankincense: Attraction, transformation, strength, blessings, honor, longevity, comfort

Myrrh: Abundance, the afterlife, balance, banishment, transformation, heartbreak, love

FOODS:

Bergamot: Assertiveness, concentration, optimism, wealth, balance

Corn: Abundance, luck, prosperity, offerings, action, balance, pregnancy

Date: Spirituality, death, rebirth, offerings, fertility, virility, healing

Grapefruit: Happiness, spirit work, cleansing, spontaneity, generosity

Kumquat: Good fortune, prosperity, rejuvenation, abundance, healing

Lemon: Cleansing, happiness, rejuvenation, clarity, friendship, youth

Lime: Purification, love, healing, protection, dissipates envy, femininity

Olive: Spirituality, integrity, passion, fertility, healing, peace, protection, luck

Orange: Love, happiness, divination, generosity, purification, clarity, fidelity

Pineapple: Protection, luck, success, prosperity, healing, hospitality, vigor

Red wine: Spirituality, offerings, happiness, love, relationships, success

Rice: Prosperity, fertility, protection, rain, grounding, issues, community, luck

Sesame: Prosperity, protection, strength, secrets, creativity, passion, luck

Wheat: Blessings, death, life, rebirth, purity, bounty, the harvest, wealth

NUTS:

Acorn: Overcoming obstacles, good fortune, protection, luck, fertility,
   eternal youth

Cashew: Prosperity, communication, wealth, love

Chestnut: Abundance, luck, justice, protection against baneful magic

Hazelnut: Beauty, luck, longevity, marriage, faeries, reconciliation,
   fertility

Walnut: Consecration, fertility, inspiration, protection, wish granting,
   transformation

SPICES:

Anise: Authority, psychic ability, emotional balance, dreams,
   home life, spirits, loss

Cinnamon: Action, attraction, business, consecration, defense, prosperity,
   love, fear

Saffron: Psychic ability, dreams, desire, the mind, fertility, passion,
   strength, happiness

ANIMALS AND MYTHOLOGICAL CREATURES:

Bear: Solitude, rest, the changing of seasons, dreams, protection, motherhood

Bee: Abundance, the afterlife, necromancy, community, purification,
   wisdom, sacrifice

Butterfly: Transformation, beauty, inspiration, opportunities, death,
   rebirth

Camel: Endurance, knowledge, trust, travel, optimism, patience, burdens

Canary: Beauty, creativity, friendship, happiness, sensitivity, blessings

Chameleon: Adaptability, psychic abilities, camouflage, creativity, patience

Deer: Peace, purification, transformation, innocence, secrets, alertness

Dragon: Ambition, destruction, protection, prosperity, wisdom, dreams, strength

Eagle: Dignity, passion, respect, courage, confidence, communication, motivation

Falcon: Beauty, clarity, growth, swiftness, strategy, strength, healing, messages

Goose: Safe travels, imagination, guidance, parenthood, home life, fertility, vigilance

Griffin: Connection, death, dignity, obstacles, partnerships, strength, guardian

Hedgehog: Concentration, defense, fertility, negativity, issues, protection, strength

Hummingbird: Balance, beauty, defense, forgiveness, messages, healing, motivation

Ladybug: Goals, happiness, luck, messages, problems, wish granting, aggression

Lion: Affection, authority, strength, pride, dignity, family, prosperity, protection, unity

Lizard: Defense, loss, intuition, growth, fear, inspiration, regeneration

Macaw: Balance, communication, creativity, emotions, visions, longevity, beauty

Parrot: Abundance, communication, wit, connection, creativity, messages

Peacock: Abundance, attraction, beauty, psychic ability, peace, death, protection

Pheasant: Awareness, confidence, determination, fertility, harmony, justice, morality

Phoenix: Beauty, new beginnings, destruction, self-improvement, knowledge

Praying mantis: Spirituality, cycles, motivation, patience, peacefulness, sacrifice

Ram: Fertility, generosity, healing, imagination, confidence, breakthrough

Rooster: Awakening, anger, confidence, courage, crossroads, death, protection

Scorpion: The afterlife, challenges, darkness, death, self-defense, protection

Spider: The afterlife, networking, danger, opportunities, wisdom, assertiveness

Swan: The afterlife, dreams, innocence, transformation, memory, secrets, trust

STONES:

Amber: Ambition, beauty, knowledge, memory, protection, longevity, healing, harmony

Ametrine: Awareness, clarity, concentration, guidance, intuition, community, decisions

Carnelian: Aggression, focus, desire, confidence, envy, protection, decisions, reversal

Citrine: Cheer, clarity, new beginnings, confidence, optimism, visions, goals, wealth

Clear quartz: Neutrality, energy amplification, activation, clarity, protection, purification

Diamond: Beauty, challenges, innocence, devotion, purification, relationships, trust

Garnet: Self-worth, heart opening, sensuality, passion, commitment, protection

Goldstone: Ambition, reorientation, self-esteem, grounding, balancing, centering

Heliodor: Courage, determination, leadership, inspiration, knowledge, willpower

Honey calcite: Amplification, confidence, courage, creativity, intuition, motivation

Petrified wood: Ancestors, protection, longevity, knowledge, rebirth, grounding, goals

Pyrite: Prosperity, protection, concentration, deceit, divination, skills, willpower

Ruby: Acceptance, balance, compassion, courage, dedication, loyalty, protection

Rutilated quartz: Meditation, insight, inspiration, development, setting intentions

Sulfur (brimstone): Transformation, banishing, protection against baneful magic

Sunstone: Action, determination, healing, growth, luck, warmth, optimism, protection

Tiger's-eye: Protection of animals, protection, wealth, travel, confidence, strength

Yellow topaz: Abundance, adaptability, affection, prosperity, courage, forgiveness

Zircon: Abundance, cheerfulness, growth, improvement, prosperity, unity, purification

METALS:

> **Brass:** Balance, deceit, healing, wealth, protection, reversal, security, returning negativity
>
> **Gold:** Authority, comfort, longevity, success, hope, confidence, wisdom, illumination

BODY PARTS:

Circulatory system, eyes, head, heart, ring finger, spinal cord

NUMBERS:

6, 36, 111, 666

COLORS:

Yellow, gold, orange, red

TAROT CARD:

The Sun

OTHER:

Mirrors

Sun Gods and Goddesses

Archaeologists have uncovered heaps of ancient structures such as megaliths, temples, and pyramids that were constructed to align with the Sun's position during the solstices and equinoxes—Stonehenge, Machu Picchu, the Pyramid of the Sun at Teotihuacan, Newgrange, the Temple Complex at Karnak, the Pyramids of Giza, and the Ajanta Caves, to name a few. The ancient city of Alexandria, established during the rule of the famed Alexander the Great, was erected in the location that aligned with the rising Sun on Alexander the Great's birthday, for whom the city was named. Possibly to harness the power of his solar return?

These sacred sites were built, wholly or in part, to worship the Sun or solar deities. A solar deity is a god or goddess who represents the Sun or an aspect of it. They are found in every culture and tradition worldwide. Many practitioners may choose to incorporate a deity in their practice, forming a relationship with them, calling upon them during spellwork, lighting a candle for them, and giving them offerings at their altar. Many of the correspondences on the earlier lists stem from these solar deities and their mythology. Let's look at some of the divine beings who have been worshipped as a solar deity or because they have an association with the Sun.

ABENAKI:

Kisosen: Solar deity, depicted as an eagle whose wings opened to
create the day.

AINU:

Chup Kamui: Lunar goddess who switched places with her brother to become the goddess of the Sun.

ARABIAN:

Malakbel: Sun god of vegetation and well-being.

AZTEC:

Huitzilopochtli: Sun god of war; often represented as a hummingbird.

Nanahuatzin: God of the Sun; sacrificed himself in fire to shine for the earth.

Teoyaomicqui: Sun god of lost souls; rules the 6th hour of the day.

Tonatiuh: Sun god and ruler of the heavens, known as "he who goes forth shining."

Quetzalcoatl: Creator god of wind and learning.

Xiuhtecuhtli: God of fire, daytime, and warriors.

BALTIC:

Saulė: Sun goddess of fertility, life, warmth, and health.

BASQUE:

Ekhi: Sun goddess and protector of humanity.

BLACKFOOT:

Napioa: Solar deity.

BRAZILIAN:

Guaraci: God of the Sun.
Meri: God of the Sun and folk hero.

CANAANITE:

Shapash: Goddess of the Sun.

CELTIC:

Áine: Sun goddess of fertility and cattle; associated with faeries, the Moon, and midsummer.
Alaunus: Sun god of healing and prophecy.
Belenus: Sun god of fire and healing.
Brigid: Irish goddess of the dawn, spring, fertility, healing, poetry, and smithcraft.
Étaín: Sun goddess of Ireland.
Grannus: Sun god of spas and healing thermal and mineral springs.
Lugh: Irish Sun god of sorcery, history, poetry, and carpenters.
Mug Ruith: Irish Sun god of storms.
Ogma: God of eloquence, inspiration, and language.

Olwen: Welsh folk hero associated with the Sun, occasionally referred to as a goddess.

Sulis: Sun goddess of healing and thermal baths.

CHINESE:

Doumu: Goddess of the Sun.

Xihe: Sun goddess, mother of the 10 Suns.

Yu Yi: God who carries the Sun across the sky.

DAHOMEY:

Mawu: Goddess of the Sun and the Moon.

DINÉ:

Jóhonaa'éí: Sun god known as "the One Who Rules the Day."

EGYPTIAN:

Amun: Creator god of the Sun, known as the "hidden one."

Aten: Sun god represented as a solar disk.

Atum: God of the setting Sun, known as the "finisher of the world."

Bast: Cat goddess of life, fruitfulness, pleasure, music, and dance.

Hathor: Sun goddess of love, mirth, and the sky; mother of Horus and Ra.

Horus: God of the sky whose right eye was the Sun and left eye was the Moon.

Khepri: God of rebirth and the rising Sun.

Nefertem: God of healing and beauty; represents the first sunlight.

Osiris: God of the underworld and king of the Nile.

Ptah: God of craftsmanship, the arts, and fertility; represents the Sun at night.

Ra: Sun god, king of the gods.

Sekhmet: Sun goddess of war, plagues, heat, deserts, and childbirth.

Sopdu: God of war and the scorching heat of the summer Sun.

ETRUSCAN:

Albina: Goddess of the dawn and protector of ill-fated lovers.

Thesan: Goddess of the dawn and new life.

Usil: Solar deity.

GERMANIC:

Sól (Sunna): Goddess of the Sun; sister of the Moon.

GREEK:

Adonis: God of vegetation and rebirth.

Apollo: Olympian Sun god of music, medicine, poetry, prophecy, truth, healing, and light.

Electryone: Goddess of the sunrise and waking after slumber.

Eos: Titan goddess of the dawn.

Helios: Titan god of the Sun, oaths, and sight.

Hemera: Primordial goddess of the day.

Hephaestus: God of blacksmiths, metalworking, craftsman, artisans, sculptors, and fire.

Hyperion: Titan god of heavenly light.

Phoebe: Goddess of the Sun; daughter of Gaia and Uranus.

HINDU:

Agni: Sun god of fire and lightning.

Aryaman: God of the midday Sun.

Mitra: God of the dawn and friendship.

Pushan: Sun god of herds and travelers.

Saranyu: Goddess of the dawn and clouds.

Savitr: God of sunrise and sunset.

Shiva: Creator god of the Moon, agriculture, art, and death.

Surya: Sun god of fertility and corn.

Tapati: River goddess of the Sun.

Vishnu: Sun god of love, protector of the world.

HITTITE:

Arinna: Goddess of the Sun.

Istanu: Sun god of judgment.

HOPI:

Tawa: Creator Sun god.

INCAN:

Ch'aska Quyllur: Goddess of dawn, twilight, and the planet.
Inti: God of the Sun.

INDIGENOUS PEOPLES OF AUSTRALIA:

Gnowee: Sun goddess who searches daily for her lost son; her torch is
the Sun.
Wala: Goddess of the Sun.
Wuriunpranilli: Goddess of the Sun.
Yhi: Sun goddess of light and creation.

INUIT:

Akycha: Sun god of Alaska.
Malina: Sun goddess of Greenland.

JAPANESE:

Amaterasu (Ten-sho-dai-jin): Sun goddess of agriculture
and peace.

KENYAN:

Ngai: Creator god of the Kamba, Kikuyu, and Maasai
peoples.

KONGO:

Ntangu: Sun god of time.

LAKOTA:

Wi: Sun god.

LUSITANIAN:

Endovelicus: Sun god of health and safety.
Neto: Sun god of war.

MĀORI:

Ao: Deity of daylight.
Tama-nui-te-rā: Deity of the Sun.

MAYAN:

Ah Kin: Sun god and protector against the evils of
darkness.
Hunahpu: One of the Maya Hero Twins; he transformed into the Sun
while his brother transformed into the Moon.
Kinich Ahau: God of the Sun.
Tohil: God of the sunrise, lightning, and
thunder.

MESOPOTAMIAN:

Baal: Babylonian supreme god of the sky and storms.

Marduk: Babylonian chief god of storms and fertility.

Nergal: God of the underworld who represents the negative aspects of the Sun.

Nusku: Babylonian god of light, fire, civilization, and the arts.

Shamash: Akkadian Sun god of justice.

Utu: Sumerian Sun god of justice.

NIGERIAN:

Anyanwu: Sun god of the Igbo, believed to dwell in the Sun itself.

NORSE:

Balder: God of beauty, light, love, and happiness; son of Odin and husband to Nanna.

Dagr: God of the daytime.

Freyr: Sun god of sexuality, fertility, peace, and married couples; brother of Freyja.

Heimdall: Watchman god of light; has keen eyesight and hearing.

PERSIAN:

Nahundi: Sun god of light and law.

POLYNESIAN:

Atanua: Marquesan goddess of the dawn.

Atarapa: Goddess of the dawn.

Maui: Folk hero associated with the Sun.

ROMAN:

Apollo: God of light, music, and healing.

Aurora: Goddess of daybreak.

Mithras: Sun god of vegetation, regeneration, and kingship.

Sol: Sun god of victory.

SAMI:

Beiwe: Sun goddess of spring, fertility, and sanity.

SLAVIC:

Byelobog (Bielbog): Polish god of light and day.

Dažbog: Sun god of warm weather.

Khors: God of the solar disk.

Radegast: Polish Sun god of war, fertility, hospitality, and crops.

TENERIFE:

Magec: Sun goddess of light, known as the "mother of brightness."

TURKIC:

Koyash: God of the Sun.

ZULU:

Umvelinqangi: Sun god of the sky, known as the "divine consciousness."

This is by no stretch a comprehensive list, but only a glimpse into the vast array of Sun gods and goddesses found around the globe. As you see, they are broken down into pantheons, but please note that some of these are closed practices or traditions that one must be initiated into. I am not an authority to educate about these cultures, nor is it my place. This information is not an invitation into someone else's culture. You must have a thorough understanding of the cultural and religious significance of the practices you use in your spirituality.

Through education, we can make more informed decisions about what is most ethical and responsible for us to use. Please be aware of the origins of the things you practice, and respect the history and people behind them. Deciding to incorporate deities into your practice is entirely your choice, and it is not a necessary part of witchcraft. The way you believe in deities is up to you, and we all have a different understanding of the divine. Because I am a pantheist, I don't view deities as conscious beings but rather personifications of nature. Pantheism is "the belief that the universe conceived as a whole is god, and conversely, there is no god but the combined substance, forces, and laws that manifest in the existing universe." This isn't to be dismissive of anyone else's beliefs but to provide context for those who may be uneasy about the subject.

I view the solar gods and goddesses as the physical embodiment of the Sun itself. As humans, it's easier for us to connect with a certain aspect of the divine when we see those qualities reflected in ourselves. It feels more natural to worship the Sun as a deity because it's familiar. It feels tangible. It gives it a name, a face. Incorporating a solar deity into your practice is another way to stay in tune with the Sun throughout the year. If you're drawn to one of the deities in the list, gather more information about them. Read their mythology, and learn about the region they came from and the followers who worshipped them there. Determine how that information can translate to your practice today in the way that feels most authentic to you.

The Solar Return Grimoire

The Sun's annual journey through the constellations provides a general framework to begin working with solar energy in your practice. The zodiac signs can be used as yet another layer of planetary timing in addition to the planetary days and Moon phases we have already covered. This next section is my personal grimoire, overflowing with spells, rituals, and simple charms to continue the momentum of your solar return throughout the year. It is divided into three distinct solar moments we experience each day: sunrise, high noon, and sunset. These all possess different energies and lessons. Sunrise and sunset are the ephemeral moments between night and day. They are both synchronously a beginning and ending, no matter how you perceive them. High noon is the peak of the Sun's intensity. It is unbridled heat beating down on the earth.

Depending on what time of day you were born, you may resonate most with the energy presented at that time because it has a personal connection to you. If you were born at sunrise, you will find the most personal power in the spells of that section. The contents were written to be created during the time they are assigned to, but they are only suggestions; do what feels best for you. For the sake of avoiding repetition, I have not included cleansing at the beginning of each working, but it is always something I recommend you do beforehand. Alongside the visualization method used in the solar return ritual on page 79, this is another way to cleanse prior to beginning any magical practice.

Solar Smoke Cleansing

MATERIALS:

- Any of the flora found in the correspondences of the Sun section, in the form of an herb bundle or incense (i.e., rosemary, cedar, goldenrod, dandelion, juniper)
- Matches or lighter

Ignite the tool of choice and then waft the smoke using your hand and say, *"By solar smoke, I cleanse this dwelling; may the Sun banish all that needs repelling."* Move it in a counterclockwise motion to banish unwanted energy from your space, yourself, and any specific objects.

Sun Water

A recurring ingredient you will find in this section is Sun Water, which, as the name may suggest, is simply water that has been infused with the energy of the Sun. It is liquid sunshine and holds the solar energy it was charged under. Depending on when you create the Sun Water, it will contain different properties. It could be the sunrise, or while the Sun was in a particular zodiac sign, or even on your solar return. Whichever time you choose is the energy it will hold. Now, how do we make Sun Water? You often hear "just set water outside," and that process doesn't make much sense to me. It feels too passive, uninvolved. I implore you to evaluate your magical belief system and ask yourself why you believe something. The answer you come up with does not matter as long as it makes sense to you.

I am an animist. I believe everything has a spirit. This is a belief system found in many religions and spiritualities, both past and present, across the globe. It is simply the idea that plants, animals, and natural phenomena possess a spirit or soul. It also may extend to include inanimate objects and things that are figuratively alive, such as spoken word. This is the essence of my craft, and it is why I believe in magic. Everything that surrounds me has a spirit I can interact with, as does the Sun. Therefore, I don't believe that if you set water outside, it will automatically become Sun Water. It requires an interaction. This is my process for making Sun Water.

MATERIALS:

+ Jar with lid
+ Water

Gather your materials. I recommend choosing a clear container that allows the most Sun to shine through. Cleanse the jar and fill it with water and then take it outside to a preferably bright, sunny spot. Stand outside in the sunshine, and lift your container toward the sky to make it look like the Sun is inside the container. Make a conscious connection with the Sun, and allow its vitality and warmth to permeate your being. Feel this energy enter the container and continue down through your fingers, letting it run through your veins. Stand there until you feel completely energized. That way, you know the Sun Water will be, too. When you are finished, audibly give thanks to the Sun. I typically leave my jar outside for a few hours afterward to really bask in that vibrant solar energy. This is a powerful magical ingredient, and there are limitless possibilities for using Sun Water in your practice. I have written specific spells that utilize it as an ingredient, which you will learn shortly, but beyond that, get creative with it and make it your own.

EASY WAYS TO INCORPORATE SUN WATER INTO YOUR PRACTICE

- Use it to represent the Sun in any spell.
- Clean with it to breathe new life into dark, gloomy places.
- Rub a drop on yourself for a quick boost of vitality.
- Drink a glass to amplify your energy.
- Wipe it on your eyes to see the truth.
- Wash your face with it for a confidence glamour.
- Add it to watercolor paints, and practice art magic.
- Water your plants or provide it to your pets for protection.
- Offer it to your ancestors or solar deities.
- Bless your magical tools with it.
- Use it for water scrying.

SUNRISE MAGIC

Each morning the darkness fades away as the Sun rises over the horizon, and the light remakes the day. The sunrise is a gift of new beginnings, a fresh start. Things are coming to fruition. We have not yet lived out our mundane lives. We are not clouded with judgments and unwanted emotions. The energy is gentle and hopeful for what is to come. However, the dark will come back eventually, and that reminds us to embrace every moment. Cast spells related to creative exploration, spiritual awakening, truth, hope, renewal, healing, happiness, second chances, self-care, peace, love, and bringing illumination and energy into your life. People born at sunrise are individualistic, initiating, determined, outgoing, interactive, and objective. They are destined to live a long and prosperous life. These are sunrise spells.

Bumblebee Sugar Scrub

A spell to rise like the Sun, to feel refreshed and recharged to take on the day.

MATERIALS:

- Mixing bowl
- ½ cup brown sugar
- ½ cup finely ground coffee
- ½ cup sweet almond oil
- 15 drops orange essential oil
- 1 drop Solar Return Oil
- Bottle of honey
- Airtight storage container

In the bowl, combine the brown sugar, ground coffee, sweet almond oil, orange essential oil, and Solar Return Oil. Use the honey to draw a bee shape in the mixture while saying, *"Honeybee, bumblebee, lend me your essence. May I be as free as thee, with an energized presence?"* This recipe makes enough for three servings and can be stored in the airtight container in the refrigerator for up to two weeks. Use this scrub following a morning bath or shower while your body is still wet. Massage it into your skin using a clockwise motion, shut your eyes, and envision it drawing warm solar energy into your being. Begin at your shoulders and work your way down to your feet while visualizing energy drawing into your being.

To Wish Upon a Sunflower

Offer your solar return talisman coin to a sunflower, and nurture it to receive your desired outcome. This is a long-term working aimed at a significant manifestation. It takes time and dedication, which allows for the best result. It is best performed on a Thursday during a waxing Moon while the Sun is in Taurus.

MATERIALS:

- 12- to 16-inch flowerpot with a drainage hole
- Drainage medium for soil, such as pebbles or terracotta pieces
- High-quality nutrient-dense potting soil
- Sun Water
- 1 seed from a dwarf sunflower variety (I recommend the lemon queen)
- Solar return talisman coin

Begin by filling the bottom of your pot with a layer of drainage medium and then pour the soil on top until it reaches an inch from the top edge of the pot.

Water the soil with Sun Water until it is completely saturated. Cup the seed in your hand, and offer it your coin, love, and affection in exchange for granting your wish. Bury the coin one inch into the center of the pot, and place the seed on top. Cover the seed with more soil, and water again. Sunflowers are a very thirsty plant, and they need to be kept in direct sunlight. Place the plant in a nice sunny area of your home, garden, or porch, preferably south facing. Water your plant with Sun Water every day and say, *"Sunflower spirit, my offering you see. Grant my wish with your petals and leaves."* As you care for your plant, your wish will grow. When it has come to fruition, or the sunflower has outgrown the pot, replant and remove the coin.

SUNFLOWER CHARMS

- To make someone be loyal to you, slip a bit of sunflower oil into their food.
- Sunflowers planted outside your home will bring good fortune.
- If you want to know the truth about something, sleep with a sunflower underneath your pillow. By the next sunset, it will be revealed to you.

Summer Berry Iced Tea

A customizable tea spell.

MATERIALS:

Berry Syrup:
- 3 cups fresh berries (Choose one berry or a combination of the berries listed below to create a tea that matches your intention set for the day.)

- 1½ cups granulated sugar
- 4 cups Sun Water

Iced Tea:
- 4 cups room-temperature Sun Water
- 6 black tea bags
- ¼ teaspoon baking soda
- 4 cups ice-cold Sun Water
- 1 cup frozen berries, for garnish

For the Berry Syrup: Rinse the fresh berries, place them in a medium pan with the sugar and Sun Water, and bring the mixture to a boil over medium-high heat. Reduce the heat to low, and simmer, stirring occasionally, for 20 minutes. While the syrup is cooking, mash the berries using a potato masher to break up large berries. This helps speed up the process, and the berries will cook much faster. Over a heatproof bowl or large canning jar, strain the syrup using a fine-mesh sieve. Discard the solids, and reserve the syrup for the tea.

For the Iced Tea: Rinse out the pan, add 4 cups room-temperature Sun Water, and bring to a boil over medium-high heat. Turn off the heat, add the tea bags, and let the tea steep for 15 minutes. Remove the tea bags, squeezing out any excess liquid, and then add the baking soda. Place the remaining 4 cups of ice-cold water in a large pitcher and then add the berry syrup and hot tea. Stir to combine, and refrigerate until ready to serve. Garnish the recipe with frozen berries. It's the best way to keep the tea cold for serving.

CORRESPONDENCES OF COMMON BERRIES:

Blackberry: Growth, protection, grieving, grounding, intuition, communication, fertility

Blueberry: Health, healing, protection, calmness, focus, faith, peace, communication

Elderberry: Spiritual protection, wisdom, spirit work, longevity, healing, abundance

Mulberry: Focus, inspiration, alertness, divination, spiritual protection, messages

Raspberry: Fun, love, courage, overcoming fear, attachments release, beauty, clarity

Strawberry: Love, attraction, beauty, desire, divination, friendship, harmony, romance

Marigold Dye

The folk name for marigolds is the "bride of the Sun" or the "summer's bride." This flower represents life and solar energy, but also death, and is often planted in cemeteries. If you've never tried naturally dyeing fabrics before, fear not, this is super easy and fun! You can use this recipe on any natural fabric—wool, silk, cotton, or linen. Dyeing clothing, veils, Tarot yarn, or cloth for your solar return altar are all great options. Not only will the fabric turn out beautiful, but it also will be imbued with vibrant solar energy and the magical properties of the marigold. This is a large recipe intended for multiple articles of fabric, but if you prefer, you can easily halve it for a smaller batch. This is best created on a Sunday during a waxing Moon while the Sun is in Libra.

MATERIALS:

- Stainless steel pot
- Room-temperature Sun Water
- 6 tablespoons alum
- 1 heaping teaspoon cream of tartar
- 1 pound natural fabric
- Bowl
- Warm Sun Water
- 1 pound fresh marigolds (not dried)

Set out all your materials in front of you, and measure out your alum and cream of tartar. Fill your stainless steel pot with room-temperature Sun Water, and set over medium heat. When the water is simmering, add the alum and cream of tartar. When they are dissolved in the water, add the fabric. Let this simmer for 1 hour, but do not allow it to boil. Remove the fabric, and add it to a warm bowl of Sun Water. Rinse the pot, fill it back up with room-temperature Sun Water, and set over low heat. Add the fresh marigolds to the pot, and let them steep for 30 minutes or until the water is orange. Remove the fabric from the bowl of warm water and add it to the pot of marigolds. (If your fabric cooled in the bowl of water, you must warm it back up before adding it to the pot. Do not put cold fabric in the warm pot of marigolds.) Stir the fabric clockwise into the pot of marigolds while saying this incantation three times: *"Sun up high, flower of gold below, sunshine into the fabric will flow."* Let the fabric sit in the marigold water until it is the color of your liking. (It will dry lighter than it appears in the pot.) Remove the fabric, place it in a bowl of warm Sun Water, and rinse the fabric until the water runs clear, adding more warm water as needed. When the water is clear, hang the fabric to drip dry.

MARIGOLD CHARMS

- A simple energy-enhancing sachet can be made with dried marigold and bay leaves. Carry it with you for enhanced vitality and protection.
- Carry a marigold on your person to radiate confidence.
- To bring prophetic dreams, sleep with one marigold under your pillow.

Haunted

This is a spell for the choices we regret. We've all done things we are less than proud of, and often, these are the mistakes we have the most difficulty moving on from. These mistakes keep us trapped in the past, haunted, incapable of moving forward and finding joy in the present. This is a spell to forgive yourself. It is best performed on a Monday during a new Moon while the Sun is in Aries.

MATERIALS:

- Old photo of yourself
- Black marker
- Matches or lighter
- White candle
- Firesafe container or cauldron

This is to be done just before sunrise. You will have to get up early to prepare. Find a location, preferably outside, where you will have a clear view of the Sun breaking over the horizon. Set up your space facing east, and lay out all your materials for the working. Place your old photo directly in front of you, and meditate on it. Turn the image over and write an inventory of all the things you have not forgiven your past self for on the back. Reflect on the time that has passed since the photo was taken, and think about how far you have come and the growth you have accomplished. Write this incantation on top of your photo: *"I forgive your choices, I forgive your words, I forgive your mistakes."* When you see the Sun peeking over the horizon, light your candle and say, *"You have taught me lessons, and they have been a blessing, but now it is a new day, and you and I must break away."* Then rip your photo in half. Take the broken pieces of your photo, light them individually with the candle flame, and carefully place them in your firesafe container to burn to ash. Finally, dispose of the ash away from your property.

Solar Simmer Pots

Also known as stovetop potpourri, a simmer pot is a bubbling pot of water and fragrant ingredients left to simmer on the stove all day. As the water evaporates into the air, the scent leaves your home smelling delightful and inviting. These four separate recipes are inspired by the seasons and significant points in the wheel of the year. As time progresses, create these different recipes to shift the energy in your home alongside the changing of the seasons. Each pot is designed to cleanse away unwanted energy and bring forth the desired. As they say—out with the old and in with the new!

Vernal Equinox Simmer Pot

MATERIALS:

- Thyme
- Chamomile

- Blackberries
- Vanilla extract
- Clover
- Lavender
- Sun Water
- Pot

Summer Solstice Simmer Pot

MATERIALS:

- Lemon slices
- Yarrow
- Daisies
- Mint
- Peppercorns
- Honey
- Sun Water
- Pot

Autumnal Equinox Simmer Pot

MATERIALS:

- Apple slices
- Cloves
- Whole pomegranate
- Garden sage

- Sunflower petals
- Pumpkin pie spice
- Sun Water
- Pot

Winter Solstice Simmer Pot

MATERIALS:

- Orange slices
- Rosemary
- Cinnamon sticks
- Mistletoe
- Cranberries
- Star anise pods
- Sun Water
- Pot

The process for creating each simmer pot is the same: fill the pot with Sun Water until it nearly reaches the rim, approximately three-fourths full. Add the ingredients for your desired recipe, set the pot over medium-high heat, and bring to a boil. Reduce the heat to low to maintain a simmer. If you replace the water as it evaporates, a single pot will last several days. When the ingredients have lost their luster, return them to the earth by burying them. I have not included measurements for these simmer pots so you can customize the recipes depending on how strong you want the scent to be and how large your pot is.

HIGH NOON MAGIC

The Sun reaches the height of its power at midday, when the rays are so overwhelming, they can be painful. Depending on where you are and what season it is, this is roughly between 12 p.m. and 2 p.m. This raw power represents true strength and the will to use it. Harness this time for more intense spells surrounding protection, control, long-term projects, fame, passion, and abundance. People born during this time enjoy a more intense connection to others. They are outwardly focused and like to engage with a broader sphere of the world. They do not enjoy spending time alone.

Here are some simple recipes to celebrate high noon magic for yourself.

Sunshine Soap

A solar infused window wash.

MATERIALS:

- 1 gallon Sun Water
- 3 lemons
- Fresh rosemary
- Bucket
- Dish soap
- Squeegee
- 3 drops Solar Return Oil
- Sponge
- Absorbent cloths

Bring a pot of Sun Water to boil over medium-high heat. Quarter the lemons and add them to the water along with the rosemary. Reduce the heat to low, and simmer for 10 minutes. Remove from the heat, allow the water to cool, and filter out the plant matter. Pour the water into the bucket, and add a few drops of dish soap along with 3 drops of Solar Return Oil. Use this mixture to wash the inside and outside of your windows. Start each window by scrubbing counterclockwise to banish unwanted energy and then switch to clockwise to seal in positivity. You can also trace personal sigils or symbols onto the window to add another layer of intention. As you clean, say *"Sacred sunlight, cleaning and purifying, grant blessings to this home of mine."*

Fueling the Flames

A witch's bottle for motivation, this is best created on a Tuesday during a waning Moon while the Sun is in Aries.

MATERIALS:

- Red marker
- Bay leaves
- Mortar and pestle
- 1 dried cayenne pepper
- Cinnamon
- Jar with a lid or cork
- Acorn or oak bark
- Matches or lighter
- 1 small red votive candle

- Firesafe container or cauldron
- Red ribbon

Begin this spell by focusing on all the things you must accomplish. Think of the goals and deadlines you must meet. Write each of these things on a bay leaf and then set them aside. In the mortar and pestle, grind the cayenne pepper and cinnamon while focusing on your intention to motivate yourself and your passions. Add this mixture to the spell jar, followed by the acorn or oak bark. Light the candle while saying, *"I am efficient, I am deliberate, I am orderly. A fire burns within me to complete goals to the greatest ability."* Individually ignite the bay leaves with the candle flame while saying out loud that you have already accomplished whatever is written on them. If one of your goals was a promotion, say "I am promoted." If one was to purchase a new car, say "I have a new car." Then carefully place the burning bay leaf in the firesafe container. After you have burned all the bay leaves, wait until there are no more smolders and add their ashes to the jar. Seal the jar with the lid, and place the burning candle on top. Allow it to burn down until it seals the jar. Tie the red ribbon around the jar, and keep the jar in a visible spot to help motivate you and keep your passions alive.

OAK & ACORN CHARMS

- Bind together two sprigs of oak with red ribbon and hang it in your home to ward off unwanted energy, strengthen familial bonds, and draw in abundance.
- Wear an oak leaf necklace to keep you from being misled.
- Carry an acorn on your person to protect against loneliness, pain, and illness.

- Should you ever find them, oak branches that have been struck by lightning are an exceedingly potent luck charm.

Confident Stride

This is a foot bath to walk with confidence, for days when you need an extra boost. Use it before job interviews, public speaking events, and first dates.

MATERIALS:

- Bathtub or washbasin
- 1 gallon warm Sun Water
- 1 lemon, sliced
- Pine needles (or pine essential oil if natural needles are not available)
- 2 cups Epsom salt
- ½ cup baking soda
- Solar Return Oil
- Lotion
- Socks and shoes
- Solar return talisman coin

Fill your bathtub or washbasin with warm Sun Water, and add the lemon, pine, salt, baking soda, and a few drops of Solar Return Oil. Place your feet in the mixture, and soak for at least 15 minutes. During that time, meditate on the tasks that lie ahead. What are you preparing for, and why are you nervous? Relax and visualize your worries dissipating through the soles of your feet. When your feet have begun to prune, remove them from the bath. Mix a dime-sized amount of lotion with 1 drop of Solar Return Oil, and rub it into your feet while saying, *"I walk with confidence, I strut with pride, I step with bravery, while my uncertainties hide."* Put on your socks, and slip your talisman coin into the bottom of one of your shoes before heading out for the day.

PINE AND PINECONE CHARMS

- Hang a pine branch over your front door to invite continuous joy inside through its evergreen properties.
- A pine branch over your bed will keep sickness at bay and support the ill.
- Carry a pinecone on your person to increase fertility, and place one at your altar to support long-term manifestations.

Return to Sender

When you find yourself on the receiving end of negative energy, this is a spell to return it to its source. This spell is directed at a specific individual who is causing you harm and will send the same amount of pain they have inflicted upon you back to them. This is best performed on a Tuesday during a full Moon while the Sun is in Scorpio.

MATERIALS:

- Photo of the individual, or paper to write their name
- Balloon
- Mirror
- Dry erase marker, preferably red

• Chime candle and holder
• Matches or lighter

To get into the right headspace for this working, you must reflect on the pain you have felt at the hands of this individual. That is the power behind the spell. Open the wounds and allow yourself to really feel these emotions. If you have a photo of this person, gaze at it while channeling this energy. If you don't, write their name on a piece of paper. Let this energy consume you; feel it boil your blood and rise in your chest, bubbling up like heartburn. Visualize it filling your lungs, and when you cannot handle holding it in any longer, blow it into the balloon. Fill the balloon with your breath, your rage, and your pain, and then knot it.

Lay the mirror on the ground, and with the dry erase marker, write and incant out loud: *"You tried to harm me. What a shame. Intentions sent are returned the same. By the mirror's reflection you must repay."* Place the photo/paper on top of the mirror, and set the candle on top of that. Light the candle. Pick up the balloon, hold it over your head, and say *"So shall it be written, so shall it be done."* Lower the balloon into the flame to pop it and return the energy to the sender.

Liquid Luck

For external use only.

Chamomile is commonly used for its properties of abundance, prosperity, and ability to increase good fortune. Folklore tells of gamblers and card players who would rub their hands with chamomile before placing bets to increase their chance of winning. To increase your luck, wash your hands with this lucky water.

MATERIALS:

- 1 gallon Sun Water
- 3 cups dried chamomile flowers
- A few drops Solar Return Oil
- Jar with lid

Bring a pot of Sun Water to a boil over medium-high heat. Add the chamomile, reduce heat to low, and simmer for 20 minutes. Strain out the flowers. Allow the water to cool, then transfer to a glass jar. Add the Solar Return oil, then store the jar in the refrigerator. This is a large batch, intended to be available anytime you need it. To use, pour some over your hands and say, *"Liquid luck, luck be mine, fortune my hands will find."*

Emerald Flames

This prosperity charm is created by lighting a bill ablaze without damaging it. This is best created on a Thursday night during a new Moon while the Sun is in Taurus.

MATERIALS:

- Water glass
- 6 tablespoons Sun Water
- 6 tablespoons rubbing alcohol
- Pinch of Borax (boric acid)
- $1 bill

- Tongs
- Long lighter

Begin by filling the water glass with equal parts Sun Water and rubbing alcohol. Add the Borax. This will transform the fire to a vibrant green when you ignite the bill and, through color magic, add another layer of energy to the working. Lay the dollar out in front of you, and fold it in half toward your body. Rotate it clockwise, and fold it inward once more. Place the folded dollar in the glass, lift up the glass, and charge it with the energy of wealth and abundance. When the dollar is completely saturated in the liquid, remove it using the tongs. Unfold it and dangle it above the glass to allow any excess liquid to drip off. With the lighter in one hand and the tongs in the other, hold the bill and light it on fire while saying, *"By emerald flame the bill is changed, charged for prosperity my way arranged."* (Alternatively, you can place the saturated bill in a firesafe container and light in there instead.) The bill will appear to be consumed by flames, but only the alcohol will actually be burning. After it has burned off, the money will remain unscathed. Carry the enchanted bill in your wallet or purse to draw in prosperity, or leave it on your solar altar to bring prosperity to your home.

SUNSET MAGIC

After burning so brightly all day, it is finally time for the Sun to turn in for the night. In its absence, we are left in a time of cold, sorrow, and death. The sunset teaches us to move on to the next part of our journey. We are closing one door and opening a new one. We are shedding the things that no longer serve us, and they are drifting into the darkness. The sunset evokes a feeling of liminality. It is betwixt and between. This is the ideal time for divination, such as Tarot or pendulum readings and spirit work. The Sun will rise again, but for now, embrace these darker energies and go deep within yourself. Cast spells related to banishment, self-reflection, healing, rest, peace, facing your fears, coping with grief, finalizing, and recovery. People born at sunset are the most reserved. They are introspective and are happiest spending time around close family and friends.

These are spells to perform at sunset.

Epiphany Dream Pillow

Herbal pillows are small pouches filled with fragrant herbs and placed inside pillowcases. Historically they were used in sickrooms to comfort the ill, alleviate symptoms, mask unpleasant smells, and soothe nightmares. This one is designed to reveal the truth. If you suspect you are being deceived, lied to, or just lacking the answer to an important question, sleep with this under your pillow to receive that information through a dream. This is best created on a Monday during a waxing Moon while the Sun is in Scorpio.

MATERIALS:

- 1 part star anise pods
- 1 part calendula
- 1 part lotus
- 3 drops chamomile essential oil
- Cloth drawstring bag

A few moments before bed, add the star anise pods, calendula, lotus, and chamomile essential oil to the bag. Lie down with your head on your pillow, and close your eyes. Hold the herbal pillow up to your chest so you may smell the herbs. Inhale their aroma and say, *"Situations are not what they appear. May my dreams reveal the truth and my path clear."* Place the herbal pillow into your regular pillow and then drift off to sleep. After you wake up in the morning and the truth has been revealed to you, store the herbal pillow on your altar. It can be reused multiple times—just be sure to cleanse it before use.

Orange Pomanders

Usually seen around the yuletide season, orange pomanders are oranges pierced by cloves and dusted with spices that, as the citrus dries, release a lovely perfume. They make beautiful decorations, air fresheners, gifts, and powerful talismans, and promote protection, good health, and fortune. This spell takes two weeks to complete, but when it is done, you will have three magical pomanders that will last a year. These are best created on your solar return, destroyed on the next, and repeated.

MATERIALS:

- 3 oranges
- 1 tablespoon cinnamon
- 1 tablespoon nutmeg
- 1 tablespoon allspice
- 1 tablespoon ground cloves

- ¼ cup powdered orris root
- Bowl
- Sewing needle
- ½ cup whole cloves
- Paper bag

Thoroughly wash and dry the oranges. Add the cinnamon, nutmeg, allspice, ground cloves, and orris root to a bowl, and set aside. Using the needle, push holes into your oranges where you would like the whole cloves to go. Be creative with the pattern. Perhaps create a pentagram, personal sigil, symbol, or constellation. When you have it mapped out, push the cloves into the holes. (This may be a bit tiresome on your fingers, so I recommend wrapping tape around your fingertips.) When the cloves are in, roll each orange in the bowl of spices and then pour all the contents into the paper bag. Every day for two weeks, shake the bag and say, *"Fortune oranges, dry, don't shrivel. Bring frivolity and frivol. Protect my home, guard this place, leaving luck in your wake."* Do not open the bag during this time. After the two weeks are up, remove the oranges and place them on your altar. Optionally, you can tie a gold ribbon around them. In a year, when they have run their course, burn them in a fire and thank them for the blessings they have provided. Remake a new set for each solar return.

Orange Divination

Before eating an orange, ask it a yes or no question and then count the seeds. If there is an even number of seeds, the answer is yes. If there is an odd number, it's no.

Cutting the Cord

This spell to permanently sever ties with another individual is best performed on a Saturday during a waning Moon while the Sun is in Virgo.

MATERIALS:

- Pen
- Paper
- 2 black candles
- 2 candle holders
- Firesafe plate
- Photo of you
- Photo of them
- Red twine
- Matches or lighter

Using the pen and paper, write a letter to the person with whom you are cutting the cord. The intention here is to never speak to them again, so get it all out. This is everything you didn't or couldn't say to them. When you're finished writing, set your letter aside. Place the candles in their holders on top of the plate, and stand them a few inches apart. One candle represents you and the other, them. Place the photo of you under your candle and the photo of them under theirs. If you do not have pictures, write your names on separate pieces of paper and do the same. Wrap the twine around both candles so they are contained together within it, and tie them together about an inch from the top. When you are ready, light the candles and pick up your letter. Read your words to the candle and photo of the individual. Yell, cry, or reflect on your connection to this person and the pain they have caused you. Release their control, and take back your power. Soon the twine between your candles will catch flame, and as it does, visualize the connection breaking between you and the other person. Say this incantation: *"I release your energy and ties that bind. Nothing connects your life to mine. The cords are cut. I am free. You have no more hold over me."* After your spell is complete, collect the ash and bury it where the Sun is setting, in the west, far away from your property.

Banishment and Blessings
Shaker Jar

This is a tool designed for a long period of use. This jar is filled with ingredients that correspond to banishing, blessing, cleansing, and the protection of home and pets.

MATERIALS:

- Dried dandelion flower
- Saint John's wort
- Bay leaves
- Lemon seeds
- Jar with lid
- Jingle bell
- Ribbon, in the color that best represents the blessings you want to bring into your home, or black for banishing

For the initial creation of this tool, add the dandelion, Saint John's wort, bay leaves, and lemon seeds to the jar. The bell, which is used for an additional layer of sound cleansing, can be added to the jar or tied to the outside using the ribbon. Screw the lid on the jar and then tie the ribbon just below the lid's lip, attaching the bell if needed. To activate the ingredients, move through your home while shaking the jar and saying, *"I cleanse this room. I banish ills from this place. With each shake, bless and protect this space."* Perform this action every Saturday to banish the old and bring forth the new for the week ahead. Store it on your altar, and be sure to cleanse the jar from time to time.

Clementine Lantern

A natural candle spell for happiness, fashioned out of a clementine. These are best created on a Sunday during a waning Moon while the Sun is in Sagittarius.

MATERIALS:

- Paring knife
- Clementine
- Firesafe plate
- Sunflower oil
- 1 drop Solar Return Oil
- Long lighter

Using the knife, carefully carve around the center of the clementine, making sure to completely pierce through the skin. Slide your fingers underneath the peel to gently remove the top and bottom, leaving you with two bowls. The peel bowl that was the bottom of the fruit will contain a pip, the fleshy bit that runs through the middle of the citrus. You will be using this as the "wick," so it must remain intact. Slowly remove the fruit so you don't not tear the pip, and set it aside. Pinch the pip to get it to stick straight up and set the bowl on the plate. Pour the sunflower oil into the bowl around the pip until it nearly reaches the top and then set aside for a few minutes while the pip absorbs the oil. In the meantime, cut a ventilation hole in the other peel bowl. This second bowl is the top of the lantern. You can cut the hole into any shape you like, as long as it is large enough for the heat to escape. Perhaps slice it into a pentagram, crescent Moon, or Sun. Return to the bottom bowl, and squeeze 1 drop of Solar Return Oil onto the pip while saying, *"Clementine lantern, holding the answer, glowing with happiness, joy, laughter. As you brighten my space, you uplift my mood, your shine forces my attitude to improve."* Light the pip. When it is steadily burning, set the second peel on top of the bottom to create the clementine lantern. It will burn for about 30 minutes, but if you would like to prolong its life span, you can add more sunflower oil as it evaporates. Sit in front of your lantern and enjoy eating the clementine fruit while focusing on improving your happiness. Alternatively, you can share this clementine with another person to improve theirs. If you must sweeten someone up, this is a great option to do so.

Twilight Tea

Use this spell to set like the Sun, to unwind and turn in for the night.

MATERIALS:

- 2 lemons
- 1 (4-inch) piece fresh gingerroot
- Blood orange
- 1 quart Sun Water
- Honey to taste

Wash the lemons, ginger, and blood orange. Cut the lemons in half, and juice them either by hand or with a citrus juicer. You will need 3 tablespoons of fresh lemon juice. Peel and slice the ginger into thin pieces. Add 1 quart of Sun Water and the sliced ginger to a small pot over high heat. Bring to a boil, reduce heat to medium, partially cover, and simmer for 15 minutes. Remove the pot from the heat, and strain the ginger-infused Sun Water into a bowl. (You can save the ginger pieces for a second batch.) Add the lemon juice and honey to the bowl, and stir to combine. Slice the blood orange into thin rounds, and place a single slice on the bottom of your mug. Pour the tea on top of the citrus to release a vibrant sunset hue, and say, *"Setting Sun, the last light, I cherish your warmth on this chilly night. You take my worries and stresses as you fade away, and I look forward to tomorrow, a bright new day."* As you sip the tea, reflect on the day you've had and envision the day you wish to have tomorrow.

GINGER CHARMS

- If you find a gingerroot shaped like a person, you can use it as a poppet, a magical doll that is bound to an individual. If you keep it safe, it will keep that person safe.
- To prevent nightmares, place a piece of ginger under the bed.
- A piece of ginger planted in a pot will invite good fortune into your home.
- To ground yourself before spellwork, drink a cup of ginger tea.
- A piece of ginger kept on your altar will increase the potency of all magical workings.

✳ SOLAR ECLIPSES ✳

The last and nearly mythical event in the Sun's schedule is something that has fascinated and terrified humankind for centuries. Before advancements in modern science, eclipses were something out of a nightmare. Historically, eclipses have been seen as life-sucking malefic omens. Our ancestors feared them and did their best to justify what they were experiencing, which gave rise to many legends of disaster and destruction surrounding eclipses. Myths of angry Sun gods and animals devouring the Sun or stealing it are found across cultures. Imagine being the first person to witness the Sun disappear. It couldn't have been a pleasant experience.

Today astronomers study these events to further their understanding of the natural world. From Earth, we can see two types of eclipses: solar and lunar. These occur when the Sun, Earth, and Moon align nearly perfectly with one another. This is called a "syzygy," derived from the ancient Greek word *syzygos*, which means "yoked together" or "conjoined." *Eclipse* is also of Greek descent. It comes to us from *ékleipsis*, which refers to the disappearance or abandonment of a celestial body.

There are three kinds of solar eclipses: partial, annular, and total. In a partial eclipse, the Moon crosses the Sun's path but doesn't completely block it out. It looks like the Sun has had a bite taken out of it, so it's safe to assume this is where the devouring myths originate. An annular eclipse takes place during the new Moon, so the Moon doesn't cover the entirety of the Sun, even if it's wholly centered in front of it, and the outer edges form a ring of fire. During a total eclipse, the Sun completely vanishes, although this is only visible from a specific part of the earth. There is also the relatively rare hybrid eclipse, which transitions from an annular to a total eclipse somewhere along its path.

The energy of the solar eclipse is robust, if not a bit overwhelming. There is some discourse within the magical community surrounding what kind of spellwork to do during this time, if any. Some believe this is an extraordinary time to manifest, while others choose to rest during this time. Deciding which camp you fall into is entirely up to you, but I did want to provide you with some context to make that decision. From an astrological perspective, during a solar eclipse, the Sun's light is destroyed. That means the new ideas that are coming to fruition are of the same destructive quality. Eclipses are like celestial atomic bombs, fueling us in a different direction. Their energy is unpredictable, and that is why some practitioners, including myself, choose not to manifest during their domination.

Eclipses are a great time to introspect and sit in receptivity with the universe. Allow yourself to be open to what it has to offer, and focus your energy on more reflective revenues. Meditate, journal, practice divination, chant mantras, take a ritual bath, or cleanse. Unless you purposely want to create chaotic energy, I wouldn't use this time to set intentions. Charging something like a talisman or water under the eclipse will also imbue it with that same energy. Therefore, unless you are trying to make a bottle of chaos, I'd avoid that.

Ultimately, it is up to you to decide what you are to do through eclipses. During the next one, sit with the energy and discern how it feels to you. If you pay attention, your body will speak to you. You may feel a little dizzy, or your thoughts may be a bit weird. You could feel completely different from how I or others feel, and that's perfectly fine. Keep track of the sign the eclipse is in, and look for correlations in that area of your life. If the eclipse is a Gemini, for example, look to the house that your Gemini is in for personal energetic shifts.

Part II

Candle Magic

CHAPTER 5

Lighting the Wick

There is something so alive about candles, from the way their flames dance on invisible winds to how you innately trust them to carry out your magic from the first time you make a birthday wish. Their little spirits work so diligently to bring us everything we desire, and each time one is lit, the world becomes a little brighter. By their virtue, we were able to survive life's harshest conditions and illuminate our way through the ages. Candles are found in all cultures' ceremonies, traditions, and celebrations, and for those of us who practice magic, they are a fundamental tool for spellwork. Candle magic is a type of magical practice that utilizes candles to assist in achieving a specific magical goal and can be performed as simply or ornately as you wish.

Elemental Candle Magic

A lit candle contains all five elements: fire, earth, air, water, and spirit. The flame itself is fire, the base of the candle that holds it steady is earth, the oxygen that sustains it is air, the wax that pools is water, and when you infuse your energy into the candle, you are spirit. When you perform candle magic, you are invoking the elements and merging them with your intention. This is the bread and butter of the practice when it's stripped of all the symbolic correspondences we are accustomed to seeing. All the elements are present in the candle, but fire is undoubtedly the most prevalent. Within elemental candle magic, the focus is on the flame. The energy you are drawing to power your spells comes from the physical element fire. This means the candle can be any color, shape, or size, and it can be used in multiple different workings. The flame is the sacred space to hold intention; the candle is only the vessel that provides it. This is an excellent way to begin your practice because you do not need anything costly, and you will learn to sense and channel energy. In a basic elemental candle spell, you only need three things: a candle, something to light it with, and a clear intention.

Representational Candle Magic

Beyond those core elements, you can incorporate whichever magical correspondences best serve your desired outcome. This is a form of sympathetic magic that entails using one thing to represent something else on the basis that like attracts like. In representational candle magic, the details matter the most because the energy is coming from the correspondences of the candle.

Each ingredient should be carefully curated to align with your intention and add power to your spell. Everything from the color of the candle, the scent, the shape, the planetary day it's burning on, the sigils inscribed into it, and the herbs it is dressed in all play a part in the working. These and more are all things to contemplate when planning a more elaborate candle spell because they determine how much energy will be empowered into the working. You wouldn't want to reuse one of these candles because the candle itself, not the flame, holds all the power. There are many ways to use these in practice. You may choose to burn them through entirely in one sitting or light them daily for a ritualistic amount of time. This can quickly become a very intricate form of magic, if not a bit complicated. Because the energy is stored within the candle, even the disposal method is crucial to the spell.

Magical Color Correspondences

Color is commonly used in all forms of magical practice, but especially when choosing the best candle for a spell. This is my personal list of color correspondences. I use it to select a candle that's most suited for the occasion.

RED

The color of the fire element, red is associated with strength, power, energy, vigor, enthusiasm, courage, protection, action, excitement, violence, lust, love, sex, romance, passion, and leadership.

ORANGE

Orange is associated with breaking blockages, opening new pathways, creativity, confidence, action, strength, attraction, encouragement, socialization, communication, new opportunities, happiness, the harvest, and legal matters.

YELLOW

The color of the air element, yellow is associated with happiness, joy, study, knowledge, wisdom, intelligence, prosperity, divination, changes, communication, travel, and mental clarity.

GREEN

The color of the earth element, green is associated with nature spirits, healing, fertility, balance, self-growth, abundance, transformation, new beginnings, good fortune, and prosperity.

BLUE

The color of the water element, blue is associated with communication, reconciliation, healing, dreams, wisdom, education, meditation, understanding, intuition, opportunity, and tranquility.

PURPLE

Purple is associated with intuition, spiritual development, magic, divination, meditation, spirit work, blessings, and psychic awareness.

PINK

Pink is associated with relationships, friendships, amplifying compassion, happiness, self-love, personal growth and success, children, fertility, family, and emotional bonds.

BROWN

Brown is associated with animals, steadiness, stability, security, roots, harvest, grounding, decision-making, concentration, and home life. Brown represents objects on this physical plane and connects you to the environment around you.

GRAY

Gray is associated with spirit communication, neutral workings, stopping situations, and undoing and stopping spellwork.

BLACK

Black is associated with breaking barriers, cleansing, protection, binding, banishing, wards, spirit communication, and justice.

WHITE

The "all-purpose color," white is associated with protection, cleansing, purification, truth, peace, meditation, enlightenment, and lunar magic.

SILVER

Silver is associated with lunar energy, meditation, psychic energy, divination, intuition, and the divine feminine.

GOLD

Gold is associated with solar energy, strength, prosperity, success, mental growth, intuition, divination, and the divine masculine.

BEESWAX

A neutral candle, beeswax is appropriate for all intentions but ideal for solar spells.

Written in the Wax

After a candle has completed its burn, you are left with the wax remains. These are treasures you have willed into existence and forged through magic. They hold the power of the spell they were created during and are an ingredient and a means to divine the future. There are messages hidden in the way the wax melts, and carromancy is the divinatory method used to uncover them. It is an easy and immediate way of revealing how that working may manifest, the amount of time it will take, what the outcome will be, and what areas of life will see a transformation. With the proper preparation, carromancy can be performed with any candle spell, including all those in this book. However, to receive the most accurate reading, there are some steps to take to limit mundane influences that could affect the results.

PREPARATION

Carromancy is best done in an enclosed room on a clean, flat surface. The wax must flow naturally and unrestricted. Don't set up near an open window where a gust of wind may sway your candle, or on a slanted table, which causes your wax to run to one side. You must have a clear workspace, such as a mirror or plate—something you do not mind getting wax on. Remove all your other tools from the area. This type of reading is ideal for pillar or votive candles and is not suitable for candles in containers. Smaller candles such as chimes and tealights are a possibility. However, they only leave behind a small ring of wax, which isn't much to read.

After gathering your materials and selecting an appropriate space for your spell, you must choose which orientation you will be working the candle from. The candle must be assigned a front, back, left side, and right side. To read the wax remains at the end, you must know this information, and the positioning must stay the same. Make marks on your plate so you don't accidentally spin your candle around.

When you are prepared for a successful outcome, it is time to perform your spell. Place your candle in the middle of the plate, and do not move it again during the duration of the burn. It must stay in the same spot and burn out completely by itself. After your spell is complete and the wax has hardened, you are ready to read the remains.

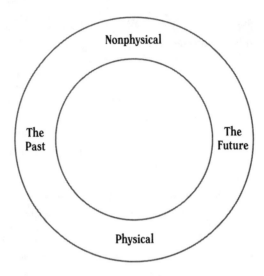

HOW TO READ WAX

In a basic carromancy reading, your candle is separated into four directions. The candle is in the center, and it represents the here and now, the current situation. It could be the day, month, or whatever the "now" of the working is. The other areas represent different aspects of life and different times.

- The top of the plate represents the things that aren't physical: mental, psychological, subconscious, and spiritual.

- The bottom of the plate represents the physical world and tangible things on this material plane: careers, finances, relationships, and possessions.

- The left of the plate represents the past, which can indicate aspects of the past that are affecting the working or that the working is helping to ease.

- The right side of the plate represents the future. It indicates how circumstances are affected by the working and what your manifested result may look like.

When you analyze these four sections together and how they relate to one another, it will give you great insight into how your spell will come to fruition. Here are some examples of what that may look like in practice:

- Imagine you do a spell to land a new job and the wax migrates to the lower right-hand corner. That would indicate both physical things and the future. Because you are divining about a possible job opportunity, I would interpret that as a positive sign you would be getting the job. Congratulations!

- If you were doing a healing spell and the wax migrated to the top left, it would indicate things that aren't physical and the past. I would interpret that as something from the past is preventing you from healing, or you need to heal a past version of yourself.

The duration the spell may take to manifest is revealed in how far the wax runs from the candle before it solidifies. The closer to the candle the wax solidifies, the sooner it will manifest in that area of your life. The farther away the wax hardens, the longer it will take to manifest. If the wax spills entirely off the plate, it may indicate that external forces will influence the spell, or that the results will only be seen far into the future. If you experience this and it's something you really desire, you need to go after it. Some spellwork takes more effort than others, and you may need to do some more work in the mundane world. If you cast that hypothetical job spell but never went to any interviews, I wouldn't be surprised if the wax ran clear onto the floor. Remember, magical responses do not manifest without earthly effort.

DISPOSING OF CANDLE WAX REMAINS

Performing a simple carromancy reading before disposing of your spellwork is immensely helpful in bringing things to the surface and seeing if there's anything you're missing. However, don't toss those remains too quickly. They have a lot of life left in them. They are a ghost of the spell they were created during and the magic still resides within them, so it's crucial that you dispose of spell remains with care. You don't want to abandon the energy you worked so hard to create. They are potent magical ingredients, primarily when used in a working to follow up the original candle spell or if you are still working on manifesting on something that hasn't come to fruition. Add them to a sachet or spell jar, or perform another candle spell on top of them.

When they have seen the end of their days, mindfully discard them while considering how they were used. Burying them is appropriate if they do not contain ingredients that may harm the earth. If they are the remains of a self-love spell or anything to do with purposely drawing in energy, bury them in your yard. Planting them in a houseplant is another option. If they are the remains of a banishment or anything to do with dispelling energy, bury them far away from your property. If this is not applicable for you, intentionally place them in the trash.

Part III

The Witch's Birthday Party

CHAPTER 6

Honoring Your Day, Your Way

Gathering with your loved ones on your birthday is customary in most places, and it's another opportunity to celebrate your special day meaningfully. In this chapter, you will find the framework to plan your own magical birthday party and to inspire you to create personal traditions. You can use this outline to throw a birthday party for yourself or another person. This is a highly individualized event and will vary from person to person, depending on their situation, so adjust the concepts presented here as needed.

The first thing to decide is location. Where will the party be? It must be somewhere you can create a sacred space because you will be performing a group ritual. There is no specific number of guests you should invite, but there must be adequate space to accommodate everyone, and they should all be people you are comfortable being yourself around. I know this isn't always applicable, but it is essential. You don't want anyone's negative energy bringing you down or affecting the working. Maybe this means the party begins with a larger number of guests who eventually dissipate into a small group of trusted individuals who will be the only ones to attend the ritual.

Preferably this party will take place on your actual birthday, but if that's not possible it's perfectly fine. Ideally, the day would be divided into two parts, the beginning spent by yourself in quiet contemplation and ending at your party surrounded by those who matter most. This would allow you to first seclude yourself to reflect on your achievements and goals and review your conduct over the past year. Examine the fragmented pieces that make your life and ask yourself what needs improvement. Are you spending time doing what you love? Are you living up to your personal expectations, or do you need to make changes?

Explore these questions and let them guide you to set your intention for the year ahead. Of course, you should have specific goals and experiences you hope to manifest, but for the group ritual, it's best to have one that is clear and concise. This is called your statement of intent. It should be simple, and it's usually the common thread that connects it all, the overarching theme. What is the underlying problem that keeps resurfacing in your life, or the one goal that encapsulates all the little ones? For example, it could be something like *"I take back control of my life and live consciously,"* or *"I am healed of my past. It does not inhibit me."* Take some time to think of yours, and write it on a piece of paper. You will need it to plan the rest of the evening. In the period before guests arrive, perform any solitary workings you'd like. Try the solar return ritual found on page 79 or the orange pomanders on page 137, or create a vision board.

The Witch's Vision Board

A vision board is a physical representation of the life you wish to manifest. It is a collage of images, quotes, and other meaningful items that you arrange on a board with the intention of bringing those things to fruition. Vision boards have made their way into the mainstream recently because regardless of whether or not you practice witchcraft, a vision board clearly represents your goals and keeps you focused on them when it is placed somewhere you will see it regularly. These vision boards are intended to be created on your birthday and set upon your altar for the following year. They are focused on the individual things you want to manifest, so be as specific as possible.

MATERIALS:

- A board
- Magazine clippings and images
- Scissors
- Markers, pens, paints
- Mod Podge
- Glue gun

These are the basic materials you will need. However, there is a lot of room for creativity. I have listed a few different options to hopefully inspire you to create something truly personal. Vision boards are usually constructed on poster board, but if you want yours to be a little more aesthetically pleasing, I recommend building it on a piece of wood or cork board. These sturdier surfaces will hold up a lot better over time and look a lot nicer on an altar. To source the images for your board, you can use magazines or print them out from a computer.

Here are some other magical materials to consider: Gather gifts from the natural world such as flowers, herbs, leaves, sticks, stones, and bark. If one of your dreams is to move to the forest, place a pinecone on your board. Suppose you wish to live by the beach; add a seashell. If you must rid yourself of a toxic relationship, collect a fallen autumn leaf. (Please be mindful of where you're collecting from because some locations are protected and have laws restricting what you're allowed to remove.) If you're feeling artsy, break out the craft supplies. You can incorporate color magic, draw sigils and symbols, or even use watercolor that's been infused by the Sun. You may want to include imagery of any specific deities you worship or items that represent them. Add crystals, Tarot or oracle cards, runes, or even candle wax remains.

As for organizing the materials on your board, consider dividing it into sections that resonate with your practice and add an additional layer of energy. If you work heavily with the elements, you could divide it as earth in the top left, air in the top right, fire in the bottom right, and water in the bottom left. Separate the materials into the element that suits them best. Say you plan to grow a garden this year. Place the representation of that in the earth section. If the board is a linear representation of things you wish to accomplish during the year, you could break it into seasons or zodiac signs. The imagery in each section could represent goals to achieve by specific points in the year.

You can create your vision board by yourself or with a group of friends. This could be a meaningful activity to do at a magical birthday party. Plus, if some of the guests are not practitioners, this is much less conspicuous than a formal ritual, and it's incredibly fun!

When you've gathered your materials, and planned out your board, use Mod Podge and the glue gun to adhere them to the board's surface.

Throughout the year, use this vision board to stay on track with your goals. By the time your next birthday rolls around, you can see how things transpired for you, and how they didn't, and direct that energy into the next board.

Group Birthday Ritual

This is the central event of the evening, a group ritual performed with your closest friends and family. It is a time to deepen your relationships by going beyond your habitual ways of relating to one another and honor your journey into the next chapter of life.

MATERIALS:

- Pillows to sit on
- Lavender bundle
- Firesafe container
- Small votive candle for each participant, in the color that best corresponds to your statement of intent, arranged on a large firesafe plate
- Lighter for each participant
- Container of salt
- Dragon's blood incense powder

Begin this ritual by forming a circle of pillows on the floor and placing all needed materials in the empty area in the center. Each participant should have a pillow to sit on and adequate space for themselves. You want to foster an environment in which everyone feels comfortable to be vulnerable and boundaries are being respected. Everyone should have a positive experience, even if it feels like a healthy leap out of their comfort zone. To create a sense of being together in this experience, sync your breathing as a group for a few minutes. Everyone should close their eyes and focus on the breath of the other individuals in the space. This will immediately connect all members through an intimate shared experience.

After the group feels connected through this exercise, it's time to cleanse. Light the lavender bundle and smoke-cleanse yourself and the materials for the ritual while saying, *"A lavender bouquet to burn the ills away, leaving only love and friendship here today."* Pass the herb bundle to the person to the left of you. They need to say the same incantation and cleanse themselves and then continue passing it counterclockwise around the circle. After each member has cleansed themself and the lavender has made it back to you, say thank you to the herb and place it down to burn out in a firesafe container.

For this next part, you may want to write a small script. Share your statement of intent with the people around you, express your struggles and dreams for the future, and tell them how they each individually play a role within that. Although this ritual centers you, the person having the birthday, it's not a one-person act. The people circled with you are your community. They are there to support you in the same way you should support them, and on each of their birthdays, you can repeat this ritual in their honor. When people gather with a shared intention, that intention is strengthened by their collective energy. Once you have verbalized your intention, be creative and follow your intuition. Be sure everyone feels welcome to share and chat about the year ahead. Tell stories, express gratitude for one another, and envision the experiences you hope to have together.

When the group has created the desired energy within the space, you will move to the circle's center so the others surround you. Pick up the plate of candles, and pass out one to each member as well as a lighter, including yourself. With a candle in one hand and a lighter in the other, say your statement of intent out loud three times and then light the candle. At the same time that you light your candle, the group must light theirs and say, *"Candlelight, candle bright, grant this wish of the night."* Return to your space in the outer circle and then place the plate in the middle so each member can set their candle on top of it.

> *"Candlelight, candle bright, grant this wish of the night."*

Next, pick up the salt container and pour salt in a circle around the plate of burning candles. After the salt has been poured, the entire group will say, *"This salt is charged with mighty force, and nothing can knock this dream off course."* Pass around the bowl of incense powder. Each member must take a small pinch. When everyone has theirs, you will throw your powder into the flames and say, *"For the benefit of all, we set this in motion now, so mote it be."* This will cause the fire to flare up for a moment and produce a twinkling effect, so allow for plenty of space. After the ritual is completed, it is time for cake!

Magical Birthday Cakes

The group ritual may be the party's main event, but the cake is undoubtedly the highlight. This is a list of popular birthday cake flavors and their correspondences. Although you may certainly choose any cake for your birthday, I recommend selecting one that supports your statement of intent. You can use any recipe you'd like and bake it with intention, or purchase something premade and charge it with these underlying properties.

Apple: Immortality, longevity, love, fertility, hidden knowledge, opening doors

Banana: Wealth, prosperity, travel, luck, male fertility, sexual stamina, divine masculinity

Carrot: Fertility, psychic awareness, sight, clarity, revealing the truth

Cheesecake: Transformation, divination, separation, success, happiness, cooperation

Cherry chip: Love, lust, divination, fertility, new beginnings

Chocolate: Romance, love, friendship, prosperity, wealth, happiness

Coconut: Purification, protection, divine femininity, female fertility

Confetti: Positivity, celebration, community, faeries, transformation, hope

Gingerbread: Longevity, perseverance, long-term goals, steady foundations

Hummingbird: Luck, prosperity, hospitality, longevity, protection, sweetening

Ice cream cake: Glamours, invisibility, transformation, cleansing, children

Lemon poppy seed: Happiness, new ventures, planting seeds, successful outcomes

Mint chocolate chip: Communication, healing a heartbreak, mental strength, wealth

Peaches and cream: Divination, warding, spirituality, harmony, motherhood, the Moon

Pineapple upside-down: Getting to the bottom of things, solving problems, wealth

Pistachio: Balance, generosity, influence, breaking curses, separation

Pumpkin spice: Protection, success, passion, determination, potency, prosperity

Red velvet: Passion, romance, lust, love, relationships, sex, remembrance

Salted caramel: Self-love, friendship, comfort, memory, clarity, protection, cleansing

Vanilla: Sweetening, abundance, gentleness, youth, sensuality, peace, dreams

Birthday Cake Blessing

When the desired cake is completed and the ritual concluded, it is time to serve.

MATERIALS:

- ◆ Birthday cake
- ◆ Candles
- ◆ Matches or lighter
- ◆ Knife
- ◆ Plates and utensils

Prepare the cake and all the materials for serving, and gather your guests around. How many candles you place on your cake is a personal preference. You could use a single candle, one for each year you are old, or a ritualistic number significant to you or your statement of intent. Light each candle and then say this blessing over the cake: *"May peace, love, and laughter be with us as we gather. Words cannot describe how thankful I am to celebrate together. Thank you loved ones, thank you Earth, for all your blessings sent forth. This event is price-less for all it's worth. I am ready to welcome in my solar rebirth. To use this year to spread positivity, joined by the bonds of family, I'm ready to make my dreams reality."* Blow out the candles and audibly say your statement of intent one last time. Use the knife to slice the cake into pieces and say, *"By the cut of the cake, magic is released, sent in all directions, north, south, west, and east."* Serve the slices to yourself and your guests, and enjoy the rest of the evening engaging in meaningful conversation.

Birthday Cake Offering

Before serving your cake to yourself and guests, set aside a small piece to use as an offering. This is a way to show your love and appreciation for the blessings you receive. The universe is constantly lending you energy for your success, and it's important to acknowledge that through a token of gratitude. Depending on your practice, you may give your offering to deities, ancestors, spirit guides, angels, etc. It doesn't matter how you see these divine forces; the message remains the same: reciprocity is critical in the same way it is in any meaningful relationship.

MATERIALS:

- Piece of cake
- Pen
- Paper

At the end of your birthday party, sit down at your altar with your piece of cake offering, pen, and paper. You are going to make a list of things you are grateful for, one for each year you have been alive. If you're 30 years old, your list should be 30 items long. These can be general, but try to focus directly on the last year of your life. Read your list out loud to the universe or the spirits you work with and then place it on the altar with the offering on top. Then say, *"I am grateful for each blessing presented to me. Thank you always. This is my gift to you."* Leave the offering on the altar for a day or two and then return it to nature. You can bury it, let it go in a river, or set it down in the woods. When you do so, say, *"Although I may discard this physical offering, the spiritual offering remains."*

A FEW LAST WORDS

Dearest Reader,

As this book draws to a close, I can only hope you have discovered more magic than you knew at the beginning. Writing it for you has been a pleasure. Once a book has been published, it no longer belongs to the author but instead to the reader. This sentiment feels even more significant given the nature of this book, and I have carried it through every page. I have pictured you in every sentence, casting every spell, brewing every concoction, and gliding your hand across the pages to fill in the blanks with pieces of yourself.

See, I told you: the people you meet, the experiences you have, the places you go, and the objects you attain are transformed by your time with them. Even if you didn't believe it, you left things differently than you found them. This book has become a synthesis of you and me. Thank you for allowing me to be a part of something so deeply personal and journeying with me until the end. I encourage you to mold the practices I have written, shaping them into something uniquely beautiful. May birthdays bewitch you and breathe new life into your practice, for the work has just begun.

NOTES

Notes

Notes

Notes

Notes

Notes

Notes

ACKNOWLEDGMENTS

From the bottom of my heart, thank you to all of those whose research, work, and support assisted me in writing this book, but especially a few select individuals: To my love, Colton, who has absolutely no interest in witchcraft and yet has read every word I have ever written. To my wonderful editor, Marian, who took a chance on me after stumbling across my social media and changed my life. To my Grandma Jeanie, who made me a nature girl. To Leah and Ella, the best witches I know and even better friends. To my father, the star watcher, who taught me about the constellations and woke me in the early hours to watch meteor showers together, memories I cherish and to which I owe my interest in the sky. To the witches of the past who paved the way for the present and future witches who will carry on the torch—or more accurately, the broom.

BIBLIOGRAPHY

BOOKS

Ahlquist, Diane. *Moon Spells: How to Use the Phases of the Moon to Get What You Want.* Avon, MA: Adams Media Corp., 2002.

Andrews, Steve. *Herbs of the Sun, Moon and Planets.* Winchester, UK: Moon Books, 2016.

Brennan, Chris. *Hellenistic Astrology: The Study of Fate and Fortune.* Amor Fati Publications, 2017.

Buckland, Raymond. *Practical Candleburning Rituals: Spells and Rituals for Every Purpose.* St. Paul, MN: Llewellyn Publications, 2002.

Cunningham, Scott. *The Complete Book of Incense, Oils and Brews.* St. Paul, MN: Llewellyn Publications, 1989.

———. *Cunningham's Encyclopedia of Crystal, Gem & Metal Magic.* St. Paul, MN: Llewellyn Publications, 2003.

———. *Encyclopedia of Magical Herbs.* St. Paul, MN: Llewellyn Publications, 2000.

DuQuette, Lon Milo, and David G. Shoemaker. *Llewellyn's Complete Book of Ceremonial Magick: A Comprehensive Guide to the Western Mystery Tradition.* Woodbury, MN: Llewellyn Worldwide Ltd., 2020.

Harrison, Karen, and Arin Murphy-Hiscock. *The Herbal Alchemist's Handbook: A Complete Guide to Magickal Herbs and How to Use Them.* Newburyport, MA: Weiser Books, 2020.

Linton, Adelin, and Ralph Linton. *The Lore of Birthdays.* Rider, 1953.

Millman, Dan. *The Life You Were Born to Live: A Guide to Finding Your Life Purpose.* Tiburon, CA: HJ Kramer/New World Library, 1995.

Patterson, Rachel. *Pagan Portals: Sun Magic.* Winchester, UK: Moon Books, 2019.

Bibliography

Tester, Jim. *A History of Western Astrology*. Woodbridge, Suffolk: Boydell Press, 1987.

An Uncommon History of Common Things. Washington, DC: National Geographic, 2015.

Zakroff, Laura Tempest. *The Witch's Cauldron: The Craft, Lore & Magick of Ritual Vessels*. Woodbury, MN: Llewellyn Worldwide, Ltd., 2017.

WEBSITES

"Archaeoastronomers Claim Alexandria Was Built to Align with Alexander the Great's Birth Date." Phys.org. Accessed October 12, 2021. https://phys.org/news/2012-10-archaeoastronomers-alexandria-built-align-alexander.html

"Artemis: Hellenic Practice and Connecting with the Goddess." Hellenion. Accessed October 12, 2021. https://www.hellenion.org/essays-on-hellenic-polytheism/artemis-hellenic-practice-and-connecting-with-the-goddess/

Mark, Joshua J. "Pharaoh." World History Encyclopedia. Accessed October 11, 2021. https://www.worldhistory.org/pharaoh/

PODCAST

Brennan, Chris. "The Astrology Podcast." *The Astrology Podcast*, June 17, 2021. https://theastrologypodcast.com/

ABOUT THE AUTHOR

Photograph courtesy of the author

Hannah Hawthorn is a pagan witch who began sharing her practice online during the quarantine of 2020. Unbeknownst to her, her content would resonate with thousands and she would amass a large following across various social media platforms under the username @simplywitched. Today Hannah continues to post in hopes of lifting the veil of misconception surrounding witchcraft and paganism, to destigmatize the craft and make it feel approachable and accessible to all. This is her debut book.